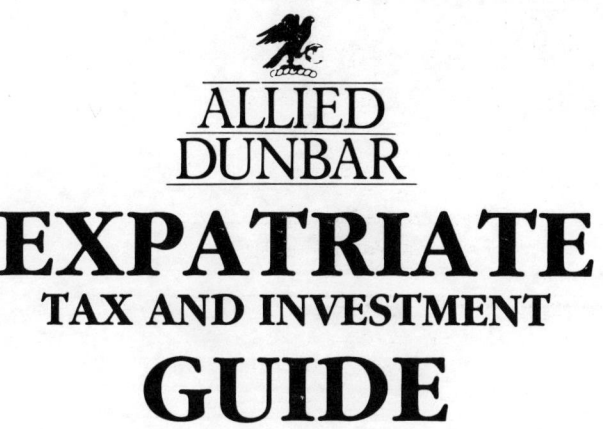

ALLIED DUNBAR

EXPATRIATE
TAX AND INVESTMENT
GUIDE

ALLIED DUNBAR

EXPATRIATE
TAX AND INVESTMENT
GUIDE

Fourth Edition

David Phillips

© Allied Dunbar Financial Services Limited 1992

ISBN 0 85121 735 4

Published by

Longman Law, Tax and Finance
Longman Group UK Limited
21–27 Lamb's Conduit Street, London WC1N 3NJ

Associated Offices

Australia, Hong Kong, Malaysia, Singapore, USA

A CIP catalogue record for this book is available from the British Library.

Printed in Great Britain by
Mackays of Chatham

Abbreviations

CGT	capital gains tax
CGTA 1979	Capital Gains Tax Act 1979
FA	Finance Act
FSA 1986	Financial Services Act 1986
IHT	inheritance tax
IHTA 1984	Inheritance Tax Act 1984
para	paragraph (of a Schedule to an Act)
s	section (of an Act)
Sched	Schedule (to an Act)
TA 1988	Income and Corporation Taxes Act 1988
TCGA 1992	Taxation of Chargeable Gains Act 1992
TMA	Taxes Management Act 1970
VAT	value added tax
VATA 1983	Value Added Tax Act 1983

Acknowledgements

The central chapters of this Guide, with their detailed exposition of United Kingdom taxation as it affects expatriates, were provided by *Moores Rowland*, Chartered Accountants, and I should particularly like to thank John Jeffrey-Cook, FCA, FCIS, FTII and his colleagues in that firm. The special chapter on tax aspects of property in the United Kingdom was written by PA Goodman, MA, ACA, ATII of *Wilkins Kennedy*, Chartered Accountants. A new chapter on investment funds has been contributed by Pauline Skypala, BA, formerly editor of *Money International* and deputy editor of *Resident Abroad*, and a new chapter on pensions by Debbie Harrison, BA, editor of the *Financial Times Pensions Handbook*. Extended coverage of international currency matters has been given in this new edition, with two chapters contributed by Howard Flight, MA, MBA, managing director, *Guinness Flight Global Asset Management Ltd*. The chapters on investment are by Richard Sayer of *Allied Dunbar Assurance plc*, with additional material by the Guide's editor. I also acknowledge with thanks the pioneering work done on early editions of the Guide by Jonathan Miller, Managing Director of *Windram Miller & Company SL*, Malaga, Spain. Finally, this edition has again benefited from the assistance of VJ Jerrard, LLB, ACII, Stuart G Reynolds, LLB, MD Davies, BA, SRC Arnot, BA, LLB, and SM Redman, LLB, all of *Allied Dunbar Assurance plc*.

David Phillips,
Editor
August 1992

Introduction

This Guide is intended to help British citizens living overseas, whether working or living in retirement, to manage their financial affairs to their greatest possible advantage. To do this it considers both current and future income, from whatever source; and assets, whether already acquired or likely to be acquired in future.

Special rules apply to the taxation of both the income and assets of expatriates, and it is the primary objective of this book to explain them. But other special factors affect expatriate finances, notably fluctuations in the relative values of various national currencies, and these factors are also explained in principle.

Our intention, in preparing this new edition, has been to make the Guide useful not only to the individual expatriate with no professional background in matters of taxation and investment, but also to professional advisers. It is to the latter category of reader, especially, that the various references to UK legislation have been addressed.

As the expatriate Briton may be residing anywhere in the world, it would be impractical to try to deal with his tax liabilities in his country of residence. But in this new edition of the Guide we have included a chapter on the basic rights and obligations of taxpayers in a number of countries, and there are likely to be analogous rights and obligations in other countries not covered here. But on matters of detail it will often be necessary to seek local professional advice.

Even as far as UK taxation is concerned, it is impossible in a book of this size to cover the subject exhaustively. Here we have tried to concentrate on the areas that we feel are likely to be of prime importance to the expatriate. For a more detailed explanation of UK tax legislation, the reader is referred in the first instance to the *Allied Dunbar Tax Guide*, the *Allied Dunbar Pensions Guide*, and the *Allied Dunbar Capital Taxes and Estate Planning Guide*; and in the field of investment to the *Allied Dunbar Investment Guide*.

United Kingdom taxation is a complicated matter, not least when it concerns British expatriates. The main reason for the complexity is that the whole present system of taxation has evolved over nearly two centuries in a piecemeal fashion, with several distinct powers, Parliament, the Treasury, the law courts, and Inland Revenue, taking part in the process.

There is a further source of complexity as far as expatriates are concerned. The various Taxes Acts and annual Finance Acts are drawn up with the habitually resident population in mind. Provisions specifically affecting expatriates are, so to speak, usually incidental to the main thrust of fiscal legislation. Case law relevant to expatriates can be cited as early as 1824, but by their very definition cases are also incidental, and proverbial wisdom has it that they are altered by circumstances. It follows that there is no systematic treatment of expatriates in what can be described only by an indulgent use of the word as the British tax *system*.

That system, such as it is, is what the Inland Revenue, tax laywers, chartered accountants, and other professional advisers have to interpret and implement. But expatriates themselves are more likely to have a different perspective altogether. For them it is more natural to consider the whole matter of tax and investment from the point of view of their own particular function — whether, in other words, they are working or retired and, if working, whether they are on a short-term contract or a more lasting arrangement, whether they are in the service of the Crown, employed by a company or a non-commercial international organisation, whether they are self-employed, and so on.

In this new edition of the Guide we have tried to clarify the subject approaching it from both these main angles: from the various categories of expatriate according to function; and from the tax system itself. But even before this can be done, there are various key terms and concepts that keep cropping up in any discussion of expatriate financial matters which are by no means self-explanatory.

So we begin the Guide with an explanation of these fundamental terms. We follow this with the two ways of classifying expatriates just mentioned. We then conclude these introductory chapters with an outline of the tax implications for expatriates, whether they are resident or non-resident in the eyes of the Inland Revenue.

Chapters 4 to 11, which follow, treat these tax matters in much greater detail, with a view to laying the foundations of sound tax planning. The tax treatment of any income an expatriate may have in the United Kingdom is first explained, a separate chapter is devoted to income from property in the United Kingdom, and further chapters deal with capital gains tax, inheritance tax, and other UK taxes. The important and highly complex subject of trusts is taken up in another chapter.

At no point in expatriate life is it more important to plan and act in advance, where tax and investment are concerned, than in the period immediately before returning to the United Kingdom, and advice on these matters is contained in a separate chapter.

The next seven chapters deal with the management of an expatriate's personal finances, and among other topics cover the construction of an investment portfolio, an explanation of the various investment media available, and the role of life assurance. Two new chapters, specially commissioned for this edition of the Guide, are devoted respectively to investment funds (including offshore funds) and to pensions for expatriates.

By definition, expatriates are highly exposed to the vagaries of the world's foreign exchange markets, and the section of the Guide dealing with international currency movements has been expanded for this edition, with, in particular, an explanation of European Community dispositions in this field.

Finally, a certain amount of reference material has been put into the appendices to the Guide, including tax tables, and a list of useful addresses.

Contents

1 Key terms and concepts in the expatriate world

1.1 Introduction

This chapter is addressed in the first place to the reader new to the subject, but it may also be useful for reference purposes to more experienced expatriates or their professional advisers.

Any person leaving the United Kingdom to spend a prolonged period overseas will soon be obliged to add a whole battery of new terms to his or her vocabulary, or at the very least, new meanings to familiar expressions. Some of these terms crop up frequently in the context of tax and investment, where they are not only specially defined but tend to have specific legal implications.

As these terms are fundamental to an understanding of the topics covered by this book, we review them at the outset. Inextricably bound up with these terms, and indeed often forming a decisive part of their definition, are a number of rules applied in practice by the Inland Revenue to determine the tax status of UK expatriates. Here we also review some of the more far-reaching of these rules.

1.2   Key terms and rules

1.2.1   United Kingdom ('The United Kingdom of Great Britain and Northern Ireland')

The United Kingdom was originally established by the Union of Great Britain and Ireland in 1801, and took its present form in 1921 when the Irish Free State (since 1949, the Republic of Ireland) was created.

The United Kingdom now consists of England, Wales and Scotland (which make up Great Britain), and Northern Ireland (Ulster). It does not include the Channel Islands or the Isle of Man, which have their own legislative assemblies and their own tax laws.

1.2.2   UK Finance Acts and Taxes Acts

The Finance Act is the annual enactment of a bill put before Parliament by the government of the day concerning the raising of finance by taxation. It incorporates the measures proposed by the Chancellor of the Exchequer in his Budget, after they have been considered in close detail in committee.

Taxes Acts either introduce a new tax, such as inheritance tax (IHT) in 1984, or consolidate previous enactments relating to a particular tax or taxes — a recent example is the Income and Corporation Taxes Act 1988 (TA 1988).

The Financial Services Act 1986 (FSA 1986) is an act of a different kind. Its purpose was to regulate the carrying on of investment business, and to make provisions concerning insurance and stock market dealings. The Act is of interest to expatriates not only because it establishes the framework of investor protection in the United Kingdom, but because it also contains provision for the recognition by the Secretary of State of collective investment schemes (unitised funds) in Member States of the European Community and in other states recognised as 'designated countries or territories'.

1.2.3 Extra-statutory concessions

These are detailed modifications to the various taxing statutes applied in general practice by the Inland Revenue. The concessions were last revised and consolidated in January 1992. Details may be obtained from HMSO Publications Centre, 51 Nine Elms Lane, London SW8 5DR.

1.2.4 UK tax year

Apparently as a consequence of the reform of the calendar in 1752, the tax year in the United Kingdom runs from April 6 one year to April 5 the next. British expatriates should be aware, however, that the tax year in their host country will be on a different basis — usually coinciding with the calendar year.

1.2.5 Expatriate

The word 'expatriate' means simply a person living away from his or her native country. It in no way refers, as is often mistakenly implied, to a person's former situation or state (there is no such thing as a 'patriate', anyway), and it is incorrect to spell the word with a hyphen.

'Expatriate' is not a legally defined term, and it is not part of the Tax Inspector's vocabulary. Instead, the Inland Revenue uses the words 'resident' and 'non-resident' (discussed below). In this book we shall henceforth follow the style of Inland Revenue leaflets by referring to individuals most often as 'he', rather than 'he or she', but only for the sake of brevity and simplicity.

1.2.6 Offshore

An asset, such as a bank deposit or shares in an investment fund, or a liability such as a bank loan is said to be offshore when it is in a jurisdiction at least one remove from that of the individual holding the asset or incurring the liability. In spite of its legal implications, however, the term is not a legal term as such, but simply one of ordinary discourse. It usually refers to a jurisdiction which, from the investor's (or borrower's) point of view, offers opportunities to mitigate tax liabilities.

1.2.7 Domicile

In 1987 the Law Commission and the Scottish Law Commission presented a report to Parliament recommending changes in the present laws concerning domicile. As far as British expatriates are concerned the proposed changes could be important, in so far as they would make it easier to establish a domicile of choice (see **1.2.10**). Interest in the Law Commission's recommendations was rekindled towards the end of 1991, when in reply to a parliamentary question the Attorney General said that the government had accepted the recommendations and would introduce legislation when a suitable opportunity arose. For a number of reasons, however, it is unlikely that such legislation will be enacted in the near future.

What follows immediately below sets out the rules in force at the time of this Guide's publication.

Domicile is a long-established concept of English common law in the first place, extended by usage to the whole United Kingdom, and it is the fundamental concept determining an individual's rights and duties. It can be defined as the legal relationship between an individual and a territory subject to a distinctive legal system. The courts of that territory may then invoke that system as the individual's personal law (relevant, for instance, to marriage and divorce, and what lawyers refer to as 'succession' — inheritance, in another word). The point about the courts is important, because many expatriates are under the misapprehension that they individually, and not the courts, are able to determine their domicile.

Put more practically, if somewhat less accurately, domicile refers to the country to which an individual belongs, the country which is his natural home. Important as it is in UK law, domicile is not a universal concept of private international law. Outside the British Commonwealth, only the United States, Denmark, Norway and Brazil use domicile as the connecting link between an individual and the system of law to which he is subject.

For British expatriates, the question of domicile is significant for reasons of tax. It is particularly important in regard to IHT, but it can also have a bearing on an individual's liability to other taxes, as we explain in later chapters.

1.2.8 Domicile of origin

While it is perfectly possible for an individual to be without a fiscal residence at any time, he cannot be without a domicile. A domicile of origin is established at birth. For legitimate children this is the domicile of the father. An illegitimate child, or a legitimate child whose father dies before his birth, takes the domicile of the mother at the time of birth. The parent's domicile will prevail regardless of where the child is born, despite any effect the place of birth may have on the child's nationality or citizenship. A child will retain this domicile of origin until he can establish an independent domicile of choice or until his father (or mother in the case of illegitimate children) himself acquires a new domicile of choice. In the latter case the child will also acquire the new domicile but this will be a domicile of dependence, not a domicile of choice.

1.2.9 Domicile of dependence

Dependency on the domicile of the parent will continue until the child reaches the age of 16 or marries, whichever is earlier (Domicile and Matrimonial Proceedings Act 1973). This does not, however, apply in Scotland where a boy can acquire an independent domicile at age 14 and a girl at age 12. Where the parents of a child under 16 (or the respective ages in Scotland) are living apart, the child's dependent domicile is that of his mother if he lives with her and does not have a home with his father.

Until 1973, a woman acquired her husband's domicile on marriage. Any woman married before 1 January 1974 will therefore have had a domicile of dependence, but she will now (following the Act of 1973 just quoted) be considered to have that domicile as one of choice if it is not also her domicile of origin. Since the beginning of 1974, a married woman has been treated as an independent person in matters of domicile and will retain her domicile of origin unless she establishes her own new domicile of choice.

1.2.10 Domicile of choice

The third form of domicile, the domicile of choice, is the one which can be of greatest interest to expatriates and which can cause the most problems. It can be very difficult to convince the courts that a new domicile has been acquired. The basic requirements are that the person should reside in the new country and that he should intend to stay there for an unlimited period. The residence part can be simply established; the length of that residence is not necessarily material, so that if, for example, a person dies shortly after arrival, he may nonetheless have satisfied the test of residence. Providing evidence of the intention to remain is more complex.

Some of the indicators of intent which will be considered on the advancement of any claim to a change of domicile include the following:

(1) a period of residence in the new country;
(2) purchase of a home there;

(3)   disposal of property in the old country;
(4)   development of business, social, religious and political interests in the new country;
(5)   burial arrangements there;
(6)   local education of children;
(7)   the making of a new will according to local laws;
(8)   application for citizenship of the new country;
(9)   severance of all formal ties with the old country.

It is invariably impossible to prove an intention; the best that can be hoped for is that the circumstantial evidence will be sufficient for the authorities to be convinced.

If a domicile of choice is abandoned then the domicile of origin revives until such time as a new domicile of choice is acquired. It would be open to the authorities to claim that on the facts of the abandonment of a purported new domicile, it did not exist. This can have serious effects for IHT if the revived domicile of origin is considered as never having been lost.

1.2.11   Deemed domicile

The 'deemed domicile' provisions contained in Inheritance Tax Act 1984 (IHTA 1984), s 267 have no counterpart in the income tax or capital gains tax legislation. The effect of this section is to treat as UK domiciled anyone who emigrates from the United Kingdom having been previously domiciled there or who had been a long-term resident. This deeming provision endures for a period of at least three years following departure.

The section treats an individual as domiciled in the United Kingdom if:

(a)   he was domiciled in the United Kingdom within the three years immediately preceding the relevant time; or
(b)   he was resident in the United Kingdom in not less than 17 out of the 20 income tax years ending with the income tax year in which the relevant time falls.

The 'relevant time' referred to above is the time at which a transfer of value takes place.

For the person domiciled initially within the United Kingdom, item (1) means there is a period of at least three calendar years from the acquisition of a new domicile during which time liability for IHT remains. For the long-term UK resident who is not domiciled here, there must be an absence of three complete income tax years before he can be free of IHT. Double taxation agreements which cover IHT may affect this provision: see Chapter 11 and Chapter 7.

1.2.12 Residence

Whatever meanings may be given to the words 'residence' and 'resident' in everyday discourse, we are concerned here only with their use in the context of UK taxation. In that context, the expressions 'ordinarily resident', 'dual residence' and 'non-resident' are also frequently used, and are defined below. None of these terms is explicitly defined in the various Taxes Acts, and the Inland Revenue states that it uses the terms 'resident' and 'ordinarily resident' in their everyday sense without giving them any special or technical meaning.

Nevertheless, the terms have been explained in a number of court decisions, going back at least as far as 1875; and the Inland Revenue in practice applies a number of rules to their application, which are set out in some detail in its booklet IR20: *Residents and Non-residents — Liability to Tax in the United Kingdom*. Most, if not all of these rules are subject to exceptions; some (but not all) of them have statutory force; while others embody certain concessions that are allowed in practice by the Inland Revenue, although not specified in the Taxes Acts. The so-called extra-statutory concessions relevant to expatriates are set out in Appendix III to this Guide.

The booklet IR20 points out that the terms 'resident' and 'ordinarily resident', while not defined in the UK Taxes Acts, are always used to describe a situation arising in a tax year (ie from 6 April to 5 April in the following year), and not in relation to some longer or shorter period. The question that generally has to be decided is whether or not a person is resident (or ordinarily resident) in the United Kingdom in a particular tax year.

1.2.13 Dual residence

An individual who is resident for tax purposes in the United Kingdom is not precluded from also being resident elsewhere, and a claim to non-residence cannot be sustained simply on the grounds of being resident in another state. A person may be resident in two or more states in the same tax year or, indeed, resident in none. Where dual residence gives rise to a double charge to tax then special provisions may exist in a tax treaty between the states which can overrule the purely domestic regulations on residence. See Chapter 11.

Finally, before going on to a discussion of the current practice, it should also be pointed out that *force majeure* will be ignored in any decision as to whether or not an individual is resident in the United Kingdom. Illness, military service, or even, in borderline cases, the cancellation of a flight, can sufficiently extend a stay so as to render the otherwise non-resident person resident for a particular tax year.

1.2.14   Physical presence: the six-month rule

If an individual is to be regarded as resident in the United Kingdom for a given tax year he must normally be physically present in the country for at least part of that year. *He will always be resident if he is in the United Kingdom for six months or more in the tax year.* **There are no exceptions to this rule** (the Inland Revenue's use of bold type). Six months is regarded as equivalent to 183 days. For this purpose a count is made of the total number of days spent in the United Kingdom during the year, whether the stay consists of one period only or a succession of visits. Under present Inland Revenue practice days of arrival and days of departure are normally ignored.

In spite of the words in bold type in the previous paragraph, the rule it refers to is subject to qualification in the case of an individual leaving the United Kingdom permanently, or leaving to take up full-time employment abroad for a period which includes one complete tax year. Such an individual may be treated as non-resident and not ordinarily resident (see below for an explanation of this expression) from the day following his departure. This treatment can be applied regardless of when during the tax year the individual leaves. If, for example, he leaves on 5 January, he will have been resident for nine months, but will be treated as non-resident for the three remaining months. This treatment is purely concessionary, but is an Inland Revenue practice of some long standing.

The converse of the six-month rule does not generally apply. That is to say that an individual who is not physically present in the United Kingdom for six months is not necessarily to be treated as non-resident for tax purposes.

An individual's residence is what lawyers call 'a question of fact'. That is to say, a question of actual circumstances. But a permanent or semi-permanent abode is not necessary to establish residence. In various court cases, a yacht, a shooting lodge and a hunting box have been held as establishing that their occupants were resident in the United Kingdom. But in other cases, living in hotels or with friends in the United Kingdom was not enough to render the individuals concerned resident for tax purposes. If an individual is physically present in the United Kingdom for less than six months, the Inland Revenue's decision as to whether or not he is resident for tax purposes depends on other circumstances.

A final point to be made about physical presence is that under TA 1988, s 334, a British subject or a citizen of the Republic of Ireland whose ordinary residence (see below) is in the United Kingdom will continue to be taxed as resident if he is abroad for the purpose of occasional residence only.

1.2.15 The three-month rule

Under this rule a person may become resident if he makes regular lengthy visits to the United Kingdom. Where the visits are made every year for four consecutive years, and the average length of stay over those four years is three months or more a year, then the visitor will be considered as resident in the United Kingdom. Where the pattern of visits is irregular or cannot be foreseen then the residence status will apply after the fourth year. If, on the other hand, the pattern is known and admitted then residence will start from the original date of arrival.

The period of three months, unlike the six months mentioned earlier, is not translated into an equivalent number of days although it can be made up of several visits. Neither is any mention made of ignoring days of arrival or departure. It would therefore seem prudent if this rule jeopardises non-resident status to keep visits to no more than 90 days per annum on average.

1.2.16 Available accommodation

If a person goes abroad permanently but has accommodation (eg, a house or apartment) available for his use in the United Kingdom, he is regarded as resident here for any tax year in which he visits the United Kingdom, however short the visit may be. A visitor who has accommodation here will be regarded as resident for any year in which he comes to the United Kingdom however short his visit might be.

Exception for full-time employees abroad: incidental duties

These two statements from IR20 are all-embracing but must be qualified by TA 1988, s 335. This section states that where a person works full-time in a trade, profession or vocation or is in full-time employment abroad and no part of his work is carried on in the United Kingdom, then his residence status will be determined without regard to any accommodation available to him in the United Kingdom. In the case of the employee, duties carried on in the United Kingdom may be ignored if they are merely incidental to the overseas duties.

The natural follow-on from s 335 is to ask what constitutes 'incidental duties'. The amount of time devoted to the incidental duties is not in itself material unless it exceeds three months (in which case they would no longer be regarded as incidental). What is important is the nature of the duties performed here and their relationship with the employment overseas. Thus, returning to the United Kingdom to report to an employer or to receive fresh instructions will usually be regarded as incidental but a director returning for board meetings would not be so treated. Other visits which are unlikely to come under the incidental duties exemption are those made by couriers or ship and aircraft crew members.

Another case which is not uncommon concerns an employee who, during an otherwise 'incidental' visit, is asked to carry out a specific task, perhaps because of some special skill he has. If he does this he is very likely to lose the protection of s 335 and be treated as resident for the year.

Availability, not ownership, is significant

Returning to the accommodation rule itself, it should be noted that it is the availability, not the ownership, of the accommodation which is significant. Thus rented property, property owned by a company or trust, or any other property which is, *in fact* available will be caught. Conversely, ownership of accommodation does not automatically mean it is available. Where the accommodation has been let on a long lease under which the owner has no right to stay there, then it is not available accommodation and will therefore be ignored. Any accommodation available to one spouse will generally be treated as available to the other.

Where accommodation is rented for temporary visits to the United Kingdom, it will be ignored if the renting is for less than two years (in the case of furnished accommodation) or for unfurnished accommodation, less than one year.

The rule does not state that the available accommodation must actually be occupied by the visitor in order that he be caught by the rule. Given also that the rule applies no matter how short the visit, it could be argued that someone with accommodation available could be classed as resident merely by changing planes at Heathrow. While for all practical purposes this possibility is remote, what is much more likely is that the person owning a property in Scotland, say, might spend a week's holiday in London and become resident notwithstanding that he never even crossed the border.

For most working British expatriates the accommodation rule does not present a problem because of s 335. However, where the expatriate is accompanied overseas by his wife he will have to take into account her residence position. If, as is usually the case, the wife is not in full-time employment, then in all likelihood, she will remain classed as resident in the United Kingdom. The question of residence is determined separately for husbands and wives. There are both advantages and disadvantages for the resident/non-resident couple, and these are discussed in later chapters.

Table 1.2   Residence summary

A person who is resident in the United Kingdom will usually have a liability for UK income tax on his worldwide income and would also be liable for capital gains on any chargeable gains.

In essence, a person will be considered resident in the United Kingdom if:

(1) he makes any visit to the United Kingdom, no matter how short, at a time when he has accommodation here available for his use unless he works full-time in a trade, etc, which is carried on entirely abroad or he is in full-time employment, all the duties of which, barring mere incidentals, are carried out overseas; or

(2) he is physically present in the United Kingdom for six months or more in the tax year, given that six months are equivalent to 183 days and days of arrival and departure are ignored; or

(3) he makes substantial and habitual visits to the United Kingdom; 'substantial' is taken to mean an average of three months or more each year and visits are considered 'habitual' after four consecutive years; or

(4) being a British subject (or citizen of the Republic of Ireland) he has left the United Kingdom for the purpose only of occasional residence abroad (TA 1988, s 334).

1.2.17   Ordinary residence

Whereas the term 'residence' is mainly concerned with individual tax years, the term 'ordinary residence' (more often encountered in the adjectival form 'ordinarily resident') implies a greater degree of continuity. Again the term is not defined in any statute, but in some relevant cases the courts have held ordinary residence to be the converse of occasional or casual residence. The Inland Revenue booklet IR20 states that 'ordinarily resident is broadly equivalent to habitually resident. If a person is resident in the United Kingdom year after year, he is ordinarily resident here'.

An individual who becomes resident in the United Kingdom under the three-month rule (see **1.2.15**) will also be considered ordinarily resident, as will the visitor with available accommodation, unless exempted under s 335 of the 1988 Act (see **1.2.16**), if he visits the United Kingdom in four consecutive tax years, regardless of how long he stays during any one visit. If an individual who has been ordinarily resident in the United Kingdom goes abroad permanently but retains accommodation available for his use there, he will be treated as remaining ordinarily resident if he visits the United Kingdom in most years. Again, the exemption conferred by s 335 applies.

1.2.18   Non-resident

An individual who leaves the United Kingdom to work full-time under a contract of employment, all the duties of which are performed abroad, and which will last for a period including at least one complete tax year, will normally be treated as not resident and not ordinarily resident from the day following his departure. This treatment remains provisional until the individual has actually remained abroad for a full tax year and, in that tax year, has not infringed any of the other residence rules.

An individual retiring abroad or otherwise permanently emigrating will also be regarded as non-resident, but the status (as with that of a working expatriate) remains conditional until a complete tax year has been spent abroad and any visits have been kept within the limits described above.

2 Categories of expatriate

2.1 Introduction

Statistically speaking, British expatriates are a fairly representative sample of the UK population at large, except that for obvious reasons their age distribution is different. In ordinary common sense terms, therefore, expatriates come in all forms and guises, and it is a mistake to think that they conform to any kind of stereotype. So in this chapter when speaking of categories of expatriate, we mean to refer only to their various situations or functions that determine their tax status in the eyes of Inland Revenue. This, we believe, is to adopt the individual's own point of view. Because in seeking a thread to guide him through the ghastly British tax labyrinth, the individual expatriate is likely to begin by defining his own situation in terms of his functional reasons for being overseas in the first place — whether, that is to say, he is working abroad and, if so, for how long and under what terms and conditions; whether he has retired abroad; whether he intends to return to the United Kingdom, and, if he does, when; or whether he has decided (or more or less decided) to emigrate permanently.

From this point on, our Guide inevitably becomes more technical, and in particular we are obliged to resort to the use of abbreviations when referring to the various Taxes Acts and Finance Acts, not to mention the occasional Inland Revenue statement of practice or its extra-statutory concessions. For an explanation of these abbreviations the reader is referred to the list on page v.

2.2 Short-term working abroad: the expatriate who remains UK resident

The previous chapter explained the terms 'resident' and 'non-resident' and it was pointed out that most working expatriates achieve non-resident status if their overseas work was for a period that included at least one complete tax year. There are, however, many people who, although abroad for more than 12 months, are not in fact overseas from 6 April to the following 5 April and who do not, therefore, qualify for non-resident treatment.

Although the expression is, literally, a contradiction in terms, we refer here to persons in this category as 'resident' (ie not non-resident) expatriates. A person in this category might, for example, have an 18-month contract commencing in June 1993; his return in December 1994 means that he has spent part of two tax years abroad but not one complete year. Then there is the case of the person whose UK job entails much foreign travel, perhaps for months on end, but whose duties in the United Kingdom cannot be described as merely incidental to his duties abroad. This category might include seamen whose voyages start or finish in the United Kingdom but who travel the world in between times. Finally, among the group of people who are abroad often but either not often enough, or not for long enough to qualify as non-resident for UK tax purposes, are the travelling salesmen, consultants, airline pilots and the like.

What all of these 'semi-expatriates' have in common is that they cannot obtain the tax benefits of the non-resident expatriate proper. They remain liable for UK income tax on their worldwide income. In the 'export or die' atmosphere of the 1970s, the importance of the semi-expatriate to the country's economic well-being was recognised and new legislation was introduced to counter the disincentive effect of domestic taxation for these people. The legislation, mainly contained in TA 1988, s 193, Sched 12, is complex and not without ambiguity. In essence, this schedule provides for total exemption from UK income tax for earnings from work done overseas provided that certain conditions are satisfied.

2.3   Long absences

Relief under this category may be obtained against earnings from an employment the duties of which are performed wholly or partly outside the United Kingdom. Any duties performed abroad which are merely incidental to those performed at home will be treated as being performed in the United Kingdom and will not be taken into account for the purposes of this relief. In order to qualify for relief as a long absentee, a person must perform the duties of his employment in the course of a qualifying period of at least 365 qualifying days. A qualifying period is not restricted by tax years and may span two or more years. For example, a qualifying period may run from September 1991 to December 1992. In that case the Schedule E assessments for 1991/92 and 1992/93 would take account of the emoluments for that part of the qualifying period in each year of assessment and grant the relief accordingly. A period of non-residence does not count as part of a qualifying period from 6 April 1992. Therefore pay for terminal leave spent in the United Kingdom following a period of non-residence would be taxable (Inland Revenue Statement of Practice SP 18/91).

A qualifying period consists either of days of absence from the United Kingdom or partly of such days and partly of days in the United Kingdom. In the former case, the situation is quite straightforward. The person performing the duties of his employ-ment wholly abroad for at least 365 days will obtain the relief. Given that the legislation refers to 'in the course of a qualifying period' there does not seem to be a requirement that the employ-ment must subsist for the whole period. Therefore an absence of 365 days made up of six months work and six months' overseas holiday would still be a qualifying period. A day will be considered as a day of absence if the person is outside the United Kingdom at the end of the day, ie at midnight (*Hoye v Forsdyke* [1981] STC 711).

The alternative definition of a qualifying period, ie where there are some days spent in the United Kingdom, contains stringent restrictions on the length of time which can be spent in the United Kingdom. Between any two periods of absence, the time spent in the United Kingdom must not exceed 62 consecutive days. Thus a person abroad for two periods of 155 days with a 60 day break between them will achieve a qualifying period of 370 days and qualify for the relief. In addition, the number of intervening days in the United Kingdom must not exceed one-sixth of the total number of days in the period under consideration. In the marginal case of a person abroad for 365 days apart from a 62 day return to the United Kingdom, although he does not break the 62 day rule, the period fails to achieve qualifying status because of the one-sixth rule. For seafarers, from 6 April 1991 the limits are relaxed to 183 consecutive days and a total of one-half (TA 1988, Sched 12, para 3 (2A)).

Employees forced to return to the United Kingdom from Kuwait or Iraq, or unable to go back there do not lose their 365-day deduction if they would have qualified but for the invasion of Kuwait on 2 August 1990 (FA 1991, s 46).

2.3.1   Qualifying periods — illustrative example

Going on from the simple case of the single return visit, qualifying periods may be built up from a series of overseas spells interspersed by returns to the United Kingdom. But what is vital with this regime is to keep a close check on the length of each stay both at home and overseas. This build-up of qualifying periods to a length sufficient to entitle the employee to obtain the tax relief is best illustrated by an example.

What the example illustrates is that the qualifying period tests have to be applied after every overseas period. An expatriate in this situation must keep a very close watch on his visits to the United

---

Example: Qualifying periods

Mr Smith is a consulting engineer who has always worked in the United Kingdom. In May 1991 he is recruited by A Ltd, an international consultancy, and is appointed to one of their projects in Nigeria for a period of 18 months. His movements over that time are given below.

Period	In Nigeria	In UK	Total
A	20	—	20
B	—	12	32
C	38	—	70 (38)⅙th=11.7
D	—	5	43
E	95	—	138 ⅙th=23
F	—	15	153
G	65	—	218 ⅙th=36.3
H	—	40	258
I	120	—	378 ⅙th=63
J	—	10	388
K	60	—	448 ⅙th=74.7
L	—	25	473
M	70	—	543 ⅙th=90.5
N	—	90	
O	40	—	40

In this example, periods A, C, E, G, I, K, M, O are all qualifying periods as they are periods of absence from the United Kingdom. None of them individually gives rise to the 100 per cent tax relief because they are each less than 365 days. Period A–C might be a qualifying period if the intervening days do not break either the 62 days or ⅙th rules. Period B, the intervening days in the United Kingdom does, however, break the ⅙th rule so A–C is not a qualifying period. As a result, periods A and B fall out of the reckoning. A new accumulation process begins with period C. C–E is a qualifying period, so too are C–G and C–I but C–I also exceeds 365 days so the 100 per cent tax relief is due. The qualifying period ceases after period M since period N is more than 62 days. A new progression can commence with period O.

Kingdom. If Mr Smith had left the United Kingdom one day earlier in period B then period A–C would have qualified.

Holidays taken abroad during a spell of overseas duty or at the end of such a spell will be included in the qualifying period. Holiday or terminal payments at the end of a qualifying period will generally also qualify for tax exemption notwithstanding that the employee might spend his terminal leave in the United Kingdom, provided the period of absence from the United Kingdom amounted to 365 days or more, but the taxpayer had not ceased to be UK resident (SP 18/91).

2.3.2   Apportionment of emoluments

The earnings or emoluments which qualify for relief are those which are attributable to the period of overseas work. Thus someone who works solely abroad may obtain exemption for all his emoluments. Where a person works partly abroad and partly in the United Kingdom (where the UK duties are not merely incidental to the overseas duties) then there is provision for the emoluments to be apportioned between the respective duties (TA 1988, Sched 12, para 2). Inland Revenue practice, however, permits relief against the whole of the emoluments unless there is some question of artificiality about the employee's arrangements with the employer (Inland Revenue letter dated 12 February 1980, reproduced in *Moores & Rowland's Yellow Tax Guide*).

The occasion on which apportionment is more likely to be a consideration is where the individual has two or more associated employments, one in the United Kingdom and others overseas. If, for instance Mr Jones, a colleague of Mr Smith, was employed both by A Ltd and A (Nigeria) Ltd, a subsidiary of the British company, and unlike Mr Smith, Mr Jones spent one year in the United Kingdom and one year in Nigeria, then if Mr Jones received a UK salary of £5,000 per annum and a Nigerian salary of £50,000 per annum he would have some difficulty in persuading the Inland Revenue that this was not an artificial tax avoidance ploy.

In any negotiations over apportionment, the amount which can be relieved is that which can be shown to be reasonable having regard to the nature of, and the time devoted to, the overseas duties in relation to the duties performed in the United Kingdom, and to all other circumstances. Returning to Mr Jones' position, he might be able to claim that his overseas duties were substantially more onerous, involved longer hours and greater responsibility, than his UK duties, that local taxes and the cost of living were far higher than in the United Kingdom and that, all things considered, £50,000 per annum was a fair rate for the job. Such a claim might well succeed. But if Mr Jones, as is not unlikely, were provided with company accommodation, car, servants and the general panoply of expatriate benefits, and received only £10,000 per annum in Nigeria with the balance paid into his UK or tax haven bank account, then his claim would be resisted with a degree of righteous cynicism.

Apportionment apart, relievable emoluments include salaries, bonuses and allowances, benefits in kind and so on. When one considers the nature of the average expatriate remuneration package with its medical cover, possible school fee payments, and other benefits as well as those mentioned earlier, the value of the tax relief becomes apparent. This, perhaps more than anything else, should ensure that the employee keeps a careful eye on his return visits.

One final point to consider about this relief is the timing of the absence itself.

For employees of companies based in the United Kingdom which operate PAYE, the relief is normally obtained by the issue of a 'No Tax' code if it is clear that the 100 per cent relief will be due.

2.4   Foreign emoluments

This term is used to describe the emoluments of a person *not domiciled in the United Kingdom* from an employment with a person or concern which is resident outside the United Kingdom. Thus, for example, an American working for an American corporation would be in receipt of foreign emoluments. Whether, and to what extent, foreign emoluments are taxable in the United Kingdom depends both on the residence position of the individual and the place in which he carries out the duties of his employment.

Duties performed in the United Kingdom are chargeable on the arising basis regardless of the residence status of the individual concerned. Where the duties are performed abroad the individual's residence is crucial. If he is non-resident then there is no liability for emoluments earned outside the United Kingdom. If he is resident but not ordinarily resident in the United Kingdom, then foreign emoluments for duties performed abroad will be chargeable on the remittance basis. If he is both resident and ordinarily resident in the United Kingdom, then the emoluments will be charged on the arising basis unless the duties of the employment are carried out wholly abroad. In this latter case the remittance basis is applied.

2.5 Other reliefs for resident expatriates

The normal rules which apply to relief for expenses, ie that they are incurred wholly, exclusively and necessarily in the performance of the duties of the employment, apply to duties which extend overseas and to the emoluments therefrom. In the usual way the expenses would be deductible from the gross emoluments and the special relief of 100 per cent would be calculated on the net amount. However, for employments which involve working overseas, certain expenses are allowable which would not be so in purely domestic circumstances. In addition, certain benefits which would be taxable in the UK employment are available with no tax penalty for overseas work.

It has already been mentioned that emoluments cover all benefits in kind and that these often form a significant part of an expatriate remuneration package. It follows, therefore, that the 100 per cent relief can cover the benefits so provided. In addition to the generality of this, there are special rules relating to travel costs, board and lodging of the overseas worker and to travel costs of the employee or his family during his spell abroad.

These rules are contained in TA 1988, ss 193, 194 and cover the following situations. In each case the employee is resident and ordinarily resident in the United Kingdom and his emoluments are not foreign emoluments:

(1) If the duties of the employment are performed wholly outside the United Kingdom then travelling expenses incurred by the employee to take up the employment and to return at the end of that employment are allowable as a deduction.

(2)   If the cost of board and lodging is provided or reimbursed by the employer this will not be assessable in the case of wholly overseas employment.

(3)   Where there are two or more employments and at least one of them is performed wholly or partly outside the United Kingdom, then travelling expenses incurred by the employee getting from one place of employment to another, where either or both places are outside the United Kingdom, are deductible against the emoluments of the second employment.

Where the expenses described above are not incurred wholly in the performance of the duties of the employment(s), they may be apportioned with relief restricted to that part related to the employment.

(4)   Travel expenses for an unlimited number of outward and return journeys to the United Kingdom by the employee are to be allowed tax free in the hands of the employee if paid for by the employer.

(5)   Where an employee is absent from the United Kingdom for a continuous period of 60 days or more, certain travel facilities will not attract any UK tax liability. These facilities are for travel by the employee's spouse and/or children under the age of 18 between the United Kingdom and the place where the duties are performed and include any accompanying journey at the beginning of the period, or an interim visit; and any return journey. These travel facilities will be tax-exempt for up to two outward and return journeys by any person in any one tax year if provided by the employer or reimbursed by him.

Several points must be noted about the reliefs described above. First, in the case of board and lodgings and the family travel facilities, the relief extends only to cases where the cost is met directly or by reimbursement by the employer. There is no relief available for the employee against his emoluments if he bears these costs himself. Secondly, the relief for travel facilities is restricted to travel to and from the place where the duties are actually performed. There is no allowance, for example, for a family reunion at any halfway house. Thus Mr Green who is working in Australia for three months could not obtain relief for a trip for himself and his family to meet up in Singapore, say. Neither his travel nor that of his family would qualify.

Table 2.1

Employees Not in Receipt of Foreign Emoluments

UK Residence Status	Employment Performed Wholly or Partly in UK		Employment Performed Wholly Abroad
	UK Duties	Overseas Duties	
Resident and Ordinarily Resident	*Case I* Earnings arising (less 100% deduction where appropriate)	*Case I* Earnings arising (less 100% deduction where appropriate)	*Case I* Earnings arising (less 100% deduction where appropriate)
Resident but Not Ordinarily Resident	*Case II* Earnings arising	*Case III* Earnings remitted to or received in UK	*Case III* Earnings remitted to or received in UK
Not Resident	*Case II* Earnings arising	Exempt	Exempt

Foreign-domiciled Employees Working for Foreign Employers

UK Residence Status	Employment Performed Wholly or Partly in UK		Employment Performed Wholly Abroad
	UK Duties	Overseas Duties	
Resident and Ordinarily Resident	*Case I* Earnings arising (less 100% deduction where appropriate)	*Case I* Earnings arising (less 100% deduction where appropriate)	*Case III* Earnings remitted to or received in UK
Resident but Not Ordinarily Resident	*Case II* Earnings arising	*Case III* Earnings remitted to or received in UK	*Case III* Earnings remitted to or received in UK
Not Resident	*Case II* Earnings arising	Exempt	Exempt

2.6　Long-term working abroad: the non-resident

In our discussion of the terms 'resident' and 'ordinarily resident' in Chapter 1, we pointed out that these terms are not explicitly defined in any of the Taxes Acts, but that the Inland Revenue claims to use them in an everyday, non-technical sense. Chapter 1 also indicated, however, that the way the Inland Revenue applies these categories in practice depends on rather complex rules.

For all that, the rules applying to the expatirate who has gone abroad to work as an employee for an extended period are to some extent simpler than those concerning other categories of expatriate. Perhaps the definition of 'long-term' is the most arbitrary part of it, because it means not simply longer than a year, but covering a complete tax year (6 April one year to 5 April the following year).

We can therefore repeat from Chapter 1 our designation of the expatriate who leaves the United Kingdom to work full-time under a contract of employment, all the duties of which are performed abroad, and which will last for a period including at least one complete tax year, as a person who will normally be treated by the Inland Revenue as not resident and not ordinarily resident from the day following his departure. This treatment remains provisional until the individual in question has actually remained abroad for a full tax year and, in that tax year, has not infringed any of the other residence rules explained in Chapter 1.

Although the treatment is provisional it does not normally prevent the Inland Revenue from making a tax repayment on departure if, for example, only part of the individual's personal allowances have been granted under PAYE. Where the year is split in this way into a resident part and a non-resident part, full allowances are due. There is no apportionment. The expatriate should obtain the tax repayment claim form P85 and submit it shortly before departure. An accompanying spouse is normally given similar treatment under Extra-Statutory Concession A78 (1992).

The main tax consequences of having the status of not resident and not ordinarily resident in the United Kingdom concern UK income tax and CGT, and are explained in detail in Part Two of this Guide. But broadly speaking, as far as income tax is concerned, the non-resident whose earnings arise from trade or employment carried on wholly overseas will have no UK liability on those earnings.

2.7 The short-term self-employed expatriate

The rules governing self-employed expatriates are not so straight-forward as those applying to expatriates under a full-time contract to an overseas employer. But here again we can usefully distinguish between those who remain UK resident under the rules and those who succeed in acquiring non-resident status.

Where the individual remains UK resident and carries on a trade or profession wholly overseas, his profits from that trade or profession are subject to UK income tax under Schedule D, Case V (see Chapter 4 for an explanation of the schedular system).

A point to bear in mind when considering profits assessed in these circumstances is that the assessment will be on the profits arising in the previous tax year, not on the profits of the accounting period ending in that year, as would be the case under Schedule D, Case I or II. Unless the overseas profits are already computed on a UK fiscal year basis — an unlikely eventuality — an apportionment of the profits will be necessary.

The profits of a trade or profession carried out partly in the United Kingdom and partly overseas by a UK resident are assessable under Case 1 or Case II in the same way as those of a purely domestic business.

A period of non-residence can be useful for an individual exercising a profession or carrying on a trade which requires his personal involvement, as the preceding year basis of assessment would be preserved on his temporary departure from the United Kingdom. Provided that an agent is not left in the United Kingdom to run the business, a person such as an author, barrister or musician who has had a very profitable year in the United Kingdom immediately before a year of non-residence will find that that income would be assessed in the year in which there is no tax charge due to his non-residence. If during the period of non-residence he is employed, the assessment would be under Schedule E on a current year basis and if he is non-resident and the duties are carried on outside the United Kingdom there will be no UK tax liability.

Self-employed expatriates also receive travel and subsistence reliefs comparable to those for UK resident employees working abroad.

2.7.1   Claims for relief

The reliefs available under Schedule E may be claimed within the normal six-year time limits, although in most cases involving substantial overseas working, the relief may be initiated by the company's PAYE office with reference to its PAYE tax office.

Relief under Schedule D must be claimed within two years of the end of the year of assessment to which the claim relates.

2.8   The long-term self-employed expatriate

In the case of expatriates who leave with no employment arranged overseas or with the intention of establishing themselves in self-employment overseas in the full sense, the Inland Revenue in effect takes a 'wait and see' attitude for up to three years. During that time a provisional status of ordinarily resident is maintained and at the end of the period, again assuming no breaking of the residence rules in the meantime, the status of not resident and not ordinarily resident may be granted and backdated to the day following departure. Any tax collected in the interim which would not have been payable by a non-resident can be repaid.

The treatment as non-resident from the day following the day of departure is concessionary (Extra-Statutory Concessions A11 and D2 (1992)), and the Inland Revenue reserves the right not to apply it in certain cases, such as where a large capital gain is made immediately after departure (see Chapter 6). Wherever a concession gives rise to a significant loss of tax to the Revenue, its application is in doubt.

2.9 Categories of expatriate

2.9.1 Expatriates with a special status

There are certain classes of expatriates who, although actually working overseas, may be deemed to be performing their duties in the United Kingdom. These include Crown servants and the armed forces, seafarers and airmen, and persons employed in exploration or exploitation activities in a designated area under the Continental Shelf Act 1964, s 1(7). The special circumstances of these individuals are described below.

2.9.2 Crown servants

The duties of an office or employment under the Crown are deemed to be duties performed in the United Kingdom irrespective of where they are, in fact, performed. The effect of this is to render the emoluments from such an employment liable to UK income tax under Case II of Schedule E if the employee is not resident and under Case I, but without any of the special reliefs, if the employee is resident. It must be stressed that this deeming provision (TA 1988, s 132(4)(*a*)) does not, of itself, affect the individual's residence position. If the Crown servant can otherwise satisfy the conditions for non-residence then the other advantages, such as no liability on overseas investment income or to CGT, will still accrue. In addition, certain allowances which are certified as representing compensation for the extra costs involved in living overseas are payable tax free. Under TA 1988, s 278 certain classes of non-resident, including Crown servants, are entitled to some or all of the normal UK personal allowances (for full details see Chapter 4 — Income arising in the United Kingdom). In practice, the Crown servant will be taxed under PAYE with an appropriate code for the personal allowances.

One exception to the UK tax liability of Crown servants concerns locally-recruited staff overseas. If they are unestablished staff who are not UK resident and the maximum pay for their grade is less than that of an executive officer in the United Kingdom on the Inner London rate, then no tax will be payable (Extra-Statutory Concession A25 (1992)).

2.9.3 Armed forces

In general terms, members of the armed forces on overseas duty are treated in the same way as other Crown servants. There is, however, one special relief available to members of the armed forces or their spouses or to a woman serving in any of the women's services. Such individuals will be treated as resident in the United Kingdom for the purpose of obtaining relief on qualifying life assurance premiums or policies issued before 13 March 1984.

2.9.4   Seafarers and airmen

Duties by seafarers and members of aircraft crews are deemed to be performed in the United Kingdom if the voyage does not extend to a port outside the United Kingdom or if the person concerned is a resident of the United Kingdom and part of the voyage or flight begins or ends here (TA 1988, s 132(4)(*b*)). This provision is now subject to TA 1988, Sched 12, para 5. This latter provision provides that seamen and aircrew engaged on voyages outside the United Kingdom are entitled to the special 100 per cent deduction for long absences (see page 14) in respect of the proportion of voyages or flights spent outside the United Kingdom. From 6 April 1991 the conditions for seafarers are more favourable: the limits on intervening days are 183 consecutive days and one-half in total instead of 62 consecutive days and one-sixth (TA 1988, Sched 12, para 3(2A)). The legislation covers two types of voyage or flight: one which begins or ends outside the United Kingdom, and any part beginning or ending outside the United Kingdom of a journey which begins and ends in the United Kingdom.

In a letter dated 22 July 1980, reproduced in *Moores & Rowland's Yellow Tax Guide*, the Inland Revenue expanded on the meaning of this provision, by quoting an example concerning the following voyages. A voyage from Tilbury to Antwerp would qualify as being carried out overseas; a voyage from Newcastle to Tilbury to Antwerp would qualify for the Tilbury–Antwerp portion; a round trip Tilbury–Antwerp–Tilbury would also qualify and that portion of a Newcastle–Tilbury–Antwerp–Tilbury–Newcastle trip would likewise be considered as overseas working. The Inland Revenue practice is that a voyage containing a scheduled call at an overseas port will have an overseas portion, but if there is no such scheduled call, then the voyage will not qualify as constituting overseas working. For the purposes of calculating the number of qualifying days for the 100 per cent relief, a person will be considered as leaving the United Kingdom when a ship leaves its berth for a foreign port or when an aircraft takes off.

Also of importance to aircrew and seamen is the question of incidental duties. It has been held that a pilot employed abroad but occasionally landing in the United Kingdom performed duties in the United Kingdom which were more than incidental (*Robson v Dixon* (1972) 48 TC 527) and in this case the pilot was treated as resident in the United Kingdom because he maintained his family home here. On *de minimis* grounds, the Inland Revenue will normally ignore a single landing and take-off during the year.

2.9.5 Oil rig workers

For tax purposes, the territorial sea of the United Kingdom is deemed to be part of the United Kingdom under FA 1973, s 38. This area is further extended in the case of employments in designated areas concerned with exploration or exploitation activities. Generally this means that persons employed in the British sectors of the North and Celtic Seas will be treated as working in the United Kingdom. 'Designated areas' are those designated by Order in Council under the Continental Shelf Act 1964, s 1(7). Apart from the rig workers themselves, this extension of the United Kingdom is also of interest to the crews of ships and aircraft servicing the offshore installations. Flights or voyages to the installations will not constitute overseas working.

2.10 The expatriate family

Many aspects of UK tax law treat the family effectively as a single unit. Thus, children's income in as much as it derives from a parental gift or settlement is treated as the income of the parent. This unified treatment ceases in the questions of residence and domicile. Not only is it the case that the residence or domicile of one spouse does not affect the residence or domicile of the other (TA 1988, s 282(2) and CGTA 1979, s 155(2)), but children are capable of having a residence status quite independent of their parents once they are no longer minors.

Because each member of a family is considered individually there is some scope for intra-family tax planning. There can also be some pitfalls if this is not done properly.

One of the commonest situations for the family of a working expatriate is that the husband (in the majority of cases) is treated as not resident in the United Kingdom from the day following departure on account of his full-time overseas employment, but his accompanying wife remains classified as a UK resident because accommodation is available in the United Kingdom (Extra-Statutory Concession A78 (1992)). Now it may be that the wife will acquire non-resident status in her own right but if the family home or any second home remains available for her or her husband's use in the United Kingdom, she will be resident in any year during which she visits there. Accommodation available to one spouse is generally assumed to be available to the other unless it can be shown that it is not, in fact, so available.

It is not uncommon for an expatriate wife to have part-time employment abroad and whether or not this is taxable, given that she remains resident for tax purposes, will depend on whether or not she satisfies the qualifying period rules for the 100 per cent relief. If she does not satisfy those conditions then her earnings overseas will be chargeable to UK income tax. Since she is UK resident she will be entitled to a single person's personal allowance.

The expatriate wife with no income of her own, either earnings or investment, is unaffected by her residence status. But if her husband has investment income arising in the United Kingdom which is liable to tax, for example, income from letting the family home, there is scope for transferring that income to the wife. It should be noted that the resident wife of a non-resident husband is entitled to the single personal allowance. This means that her allowance can be used to offset investment income, resulting perhaps in a repayment of tax credit or of income tax deducted at source. It is important, however, that income-producing assets should be held in one name only if the income would be exempt in the husband's case. A joint bank deposit account where one of the parties is resident will produce interest all of which is liable to UK tax, whereas a sole account held by the non-resident party would result in the liability not being pursued in view of Extra-Statutory Concession B13 (1992) (see also Chapter 14).

The general rule is that UK assets producing taxable income should be held by the resident spouse and UK assets producing an income exempt in the hands of a non-resident and non-UK assets should be held by the non-resident spouse.

Independent taxation means that spouses are also treated separately for capital gains tax (CGT), each having a small gains exemption (£5,800 for 1992/93, SI 1992 No 626).

Children who remain resident in the United Kingdom, perhaps staying at a boarding school, are also entitled to a personal allowance. Where the parents are resident in the United Kingdom this personal allowance of the children is rarely of significant benefit unless the child has a substantial income from a non-parental source. Gifts from parents to children are treated as settlements and any income arising therefrom is treated as if it were the parent's income. This does not apply, however, where the parent is not resident in the United Kingdom (TA 1988, s 663(5)). Because of this, a parent might usefully make a gift of certain income-producing assets to his children who would then be able to claim relief against that income. The tax repayment might, for example, go some way towards paying for school fees, etc. Provided that this were an outright gift to the child there should be no charge to IHT.

On the parent's return to UK resident status, any continuing income from the gift would revert to being taxed as that of the parent until the child reached age 18, or, if earlier, until he or she married.

2.11 Expatriates retiring abroad or permanently emigrating

The Inland Revenue treatment of persons retiring abroad or otherwise permanently emigrating is very much the same as that given to a temporary expatriate taking up overseas employment and the non-resident status remains conditional until a complete tax year has been spent abroad and any visits have been kept within the limits described in Chapter 1. Confirmation of the non-resident status is rarely, in fact, given, unless the emigrant has cause to continue to complete UK tax returns because of continuing UK income sources. Although an enquiry might be made of the emigrant to determine whether or not he remains non-resident after the first tax year, as often as not this is a futile enquiry and his tax office file will eventually become a dead file. The Inland Revenue does, however, have remarkable powers of recovering files, if not the individuals they relate to, from limbo. The dead file will normally be traced should the emigrant decide to return to the United Kingdom.

It would be normal for most people leaving permanently to sell their home in the United Kingdom and this is considered as quite firm evidence of intent by the Inland Revenue. It is by no means crucial for the emigrant who has employment arranged in his new country, because he will in any case be treated as any other overseas employed expatriate.

2.11.1 The retired expatriate

But in the case of a retired emigrant or one who is self-employed, failure to divest himself of his property in this country will mean that he will continue to be regarded provisionally as resident and ordinarily resident for up to three years after departure. A decision on his resident status will be made retrospectively in the light of what has actually happened in the meantime. During the three intervening years, his tax liability will be provisionally computed on the basis that he remains resident in the United Kingdom. Such a person will also have a provisional entitlement to personal allowances (since he is provisionally resident) and these will be reflected in any PAYE code operated, for example, against a company pension, or may form the basis of a tax repayment claim if tax is deducted, or effectively deducted in the form of tax credits, from interest, dividends, or other sources of income.

If the emigrant is not working full-time in an employment, trade, or profession abroad, then retaining his UK property can be particularly dangerous. If it is available for his use, then he need only set foot in the United Kingdom in a tax year to become resident for that year. Unless, that is, there is a double taxation agreement between his new country and the United Kingdom which overrides this provision.

If after three years the emigrant has not broken the rules, then his non-resident, non-ordinarily resident status will normally be back-dated to the day following his departure. Any tax paid in the meantime because of his provisionally resident treatment which would not have been payable in the case of a non-resident will then be repaid.

3 Guide to domicile and residence: the tax consequences

3.1 Introduction

Based on the concepts of domicile and residence explained in the two preceding chapters, this chapter is intended as a schematic guide to the tax and investment planning chapters that follow it. It is intended, therefore, as a bridge between the definitions and categories established in the previous chapters and the detailed exposition of tax matters, particularly, in the subsequent chapters of this book. In the tabular form in which it is presented, the guide leads only to general conclusions and strategies. **It is not a rule-book**, but is simply intended to point in the right direction. In using this guide, it is important **to check the status of each spouse separately**, in order to identify the relevant category.

3.2 Using the guide

Step 1: establish domicile

Use Domicile Chart as guide

For IHT purposes **only**, it is possible for the Revenue to **deem** an individual UK domiciled (such action does not disturb the legal domicile).

Step 2: establish where resident for tax purposes

Use:

Resident Chart 1 for non-UK domiciled client
Resident Chart 2 for working UK expatriates
Resident Chart 3 for non-working UK expatriates.

Step 3: check tax and investment considerations

Having decided domicile and residence category, use:

(1)   UK Taxation Chart to check planned actions for tax effectiveness
(2)   UK Taxation — Effect on Investment, etc to check overall financial strategy*

The symbols on this chart can be regarded as:

☺   Usually 'harmless', or even good!

⑦   May well be harmless but take care to double check

⚠   Check — there could be disadvantages

🛑   Check carefully — there will usually be major disadvantages

Ensure no conflict with sensible tax and investment planning.

Category: A

Applies to:
Non-UK Domicile
Non-UK Resident
Non-UK Ordinarily Resident

Basic strategy:
Can invest in the United Kingdom provided local legal and exchange controls permit. To minimise risk of IHT on UK assets, should:

(1)   restrict UK assets below IHT zero-rated band
(2)   take advantage of HM Government exempt stocks
(3)   ensure any 'portable' assets are held outside the United Kingdom

Also, of IHT advantage and effective in reducing UK withholding tax, are the investments offered by offshore subsidiaries of UK institutions, which can offer UK investment qualities without UK taxation.

Category: B

Applies to:
Non-UK Domicile
UK Resident
UK Ordinarily Resident

Basic strategy:
To minimise UK tax liabilities should keep all assets and accumulated gains/income outside the United Kingdom, remitting to the United Kingdom **only** the absolute minimum. If remittance, to cover living expenses, is unavoidable, client should create separate accounts to contain and identify:

(1) income arising outside the United Kingdom
(2) gain-laden capital from asset disposal
(3) capital untainted by income or gain.

Remittance could be from (2) up to limit of CGT exemptions in any one year; if more cash is required, remittance could be made from (3); only in the direst straits should cash be remitted from (1).

Category: C

Applies to:
UK Domicile
Non-UK Resident
Non-UK Ordinarily Resident

Basic strategy:
Invest in offshore subsidiaries of UK institutions, to retain investment qualities without unnecessary UK tax implications. Ensure spare capital is working for capital growth as well as income, and realise all accumulated capital gains while still non-UK ordinarily resident.

Take care to maintain a realistic level of health insurance and life cover and keep equal cover for a spouse running the UK family base, if appropriate.

If one spouse remains UK resident, take care to avoid **joint** assets, as the income/gain on the asset will be assessable to UK taxes.

Category: D

Applies to:
UK Domicile (but claiming new domicile of choice)
Non-UK Resident
Non-UK Ordinarily Resident

Basic strategy:
As part of exercise to replace UK domicile with new domicile of choice, the individual concerned must show that all formal ties with the United Kingdom have been severed. Single 'ties', eg a banking service, an investment in a UK equity, etc, will not individually prevent a successful claim to non-UK domicile, but together could convince the UK authorities that the client retains British roots.

Should, therefore, move everything possible offshore and use UK facilities only if quite sure it will not damage non-domicile claim.

It may be a wise precaution to plan for eventual IHT liability, on the assumption that the claim may eventually fail.

Note:
An expatriate will be treated as deemed domiciled (for IHT purposes only) for first three years following departure.

Domicile and residence charts start on page 36.

Domicile Chart

UK domiciled or Non-UK Domiciled?

Note: If 'domicile of choice' not **actively** established, domicile will be either 'domicile of origin' or 'domicile of dependence'.

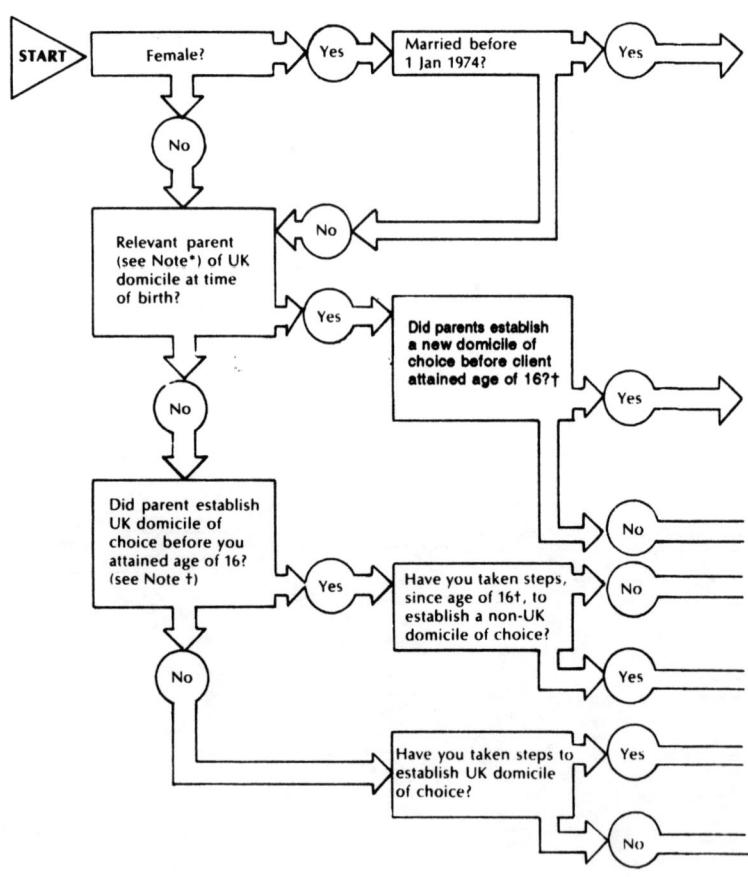

Note*: If parents were married (to each other!) at
        time of birth, take father as relevant parent:
        otherwise, take mother as relevant parent.
Note†: Except in Scotland, where the
        relevant age is 14 for males
        and 12 for females.

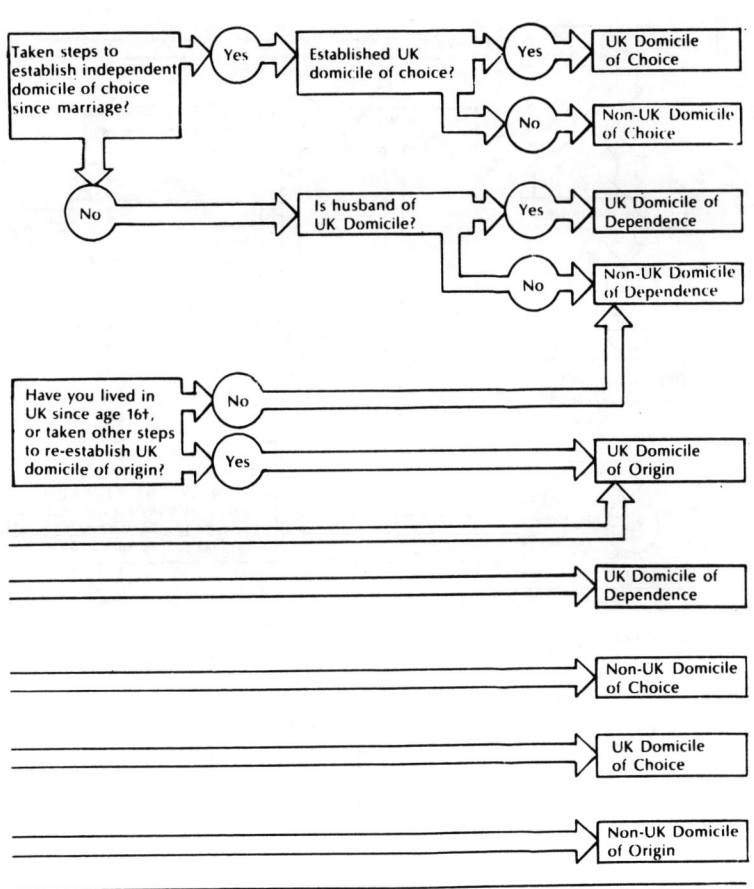

Residence Chart-1 (Non-UK Domicile)
Non-UK Domiciled ie

Roots, parentage etc outside UK

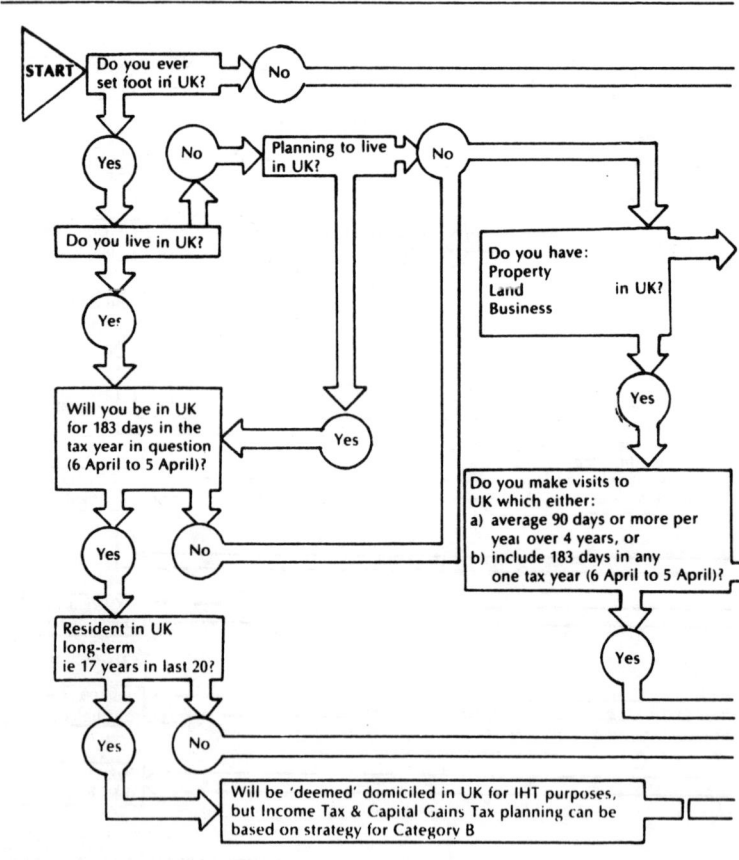

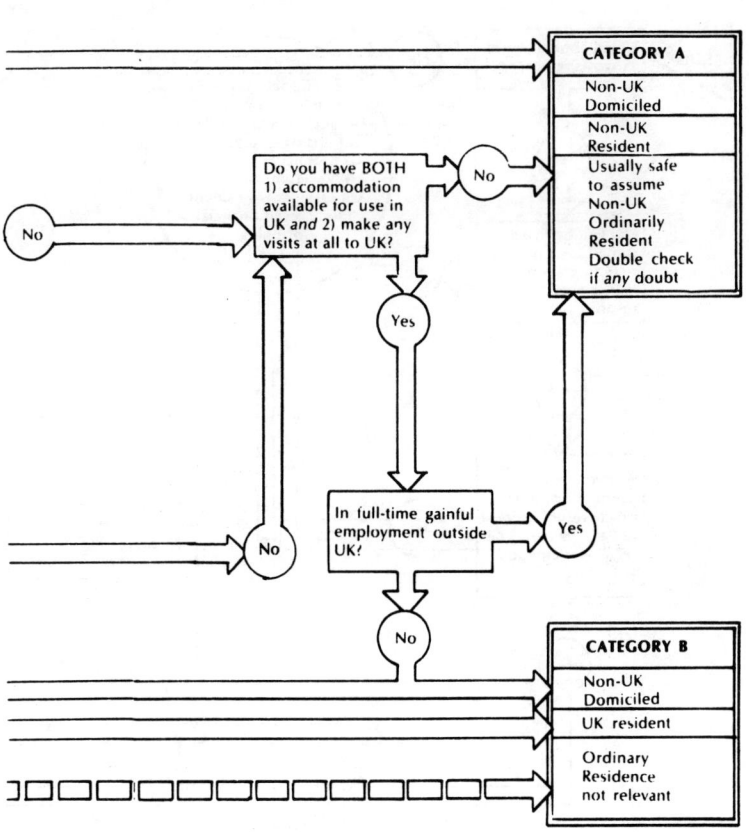

Residence Chart-2 (UK Domicile Employed)
Non-UK Domiciled working abroad ie

Roots, parentage etc (domicile) in UK, and in
full-time gainful occupation outside UK.

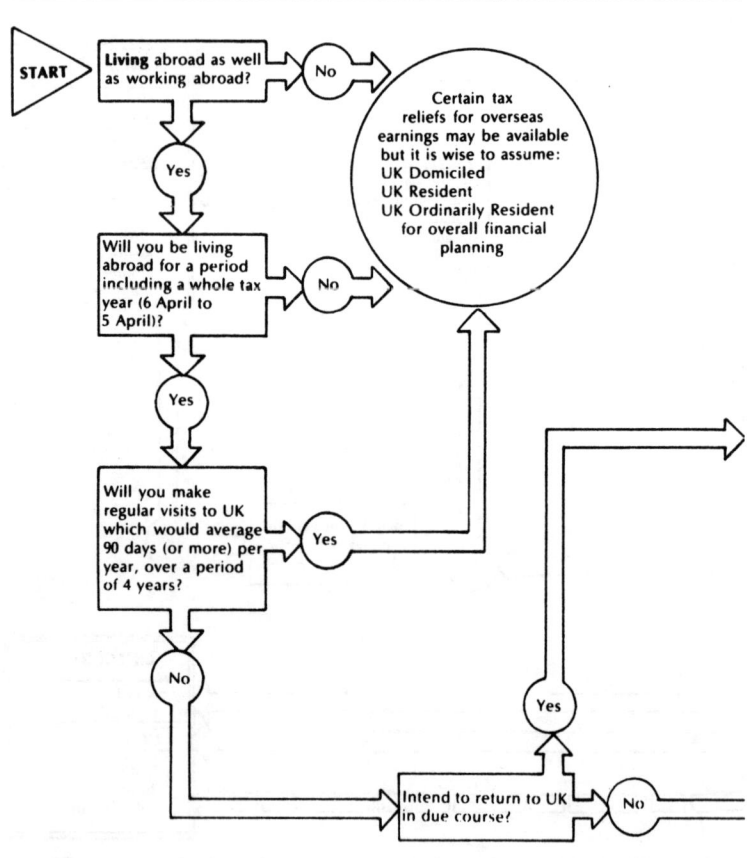

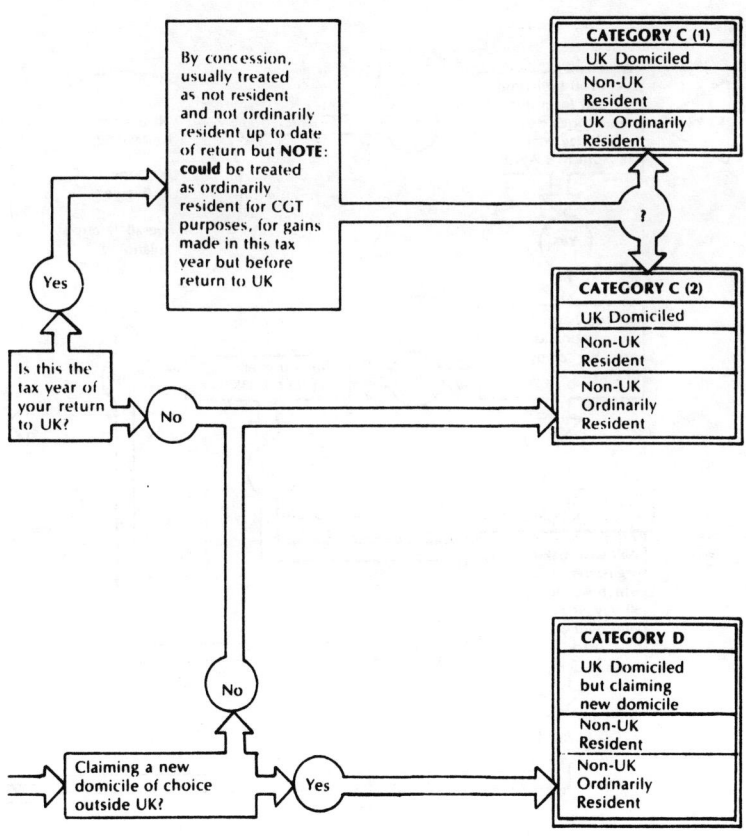

Residence Chart-3 (UK Domicile-Not Employed)

UK-Domiciled living abroad ie

Roots, parentage etc (domicile) in UK, living
outside UK, but not in full-time gainful occupation.

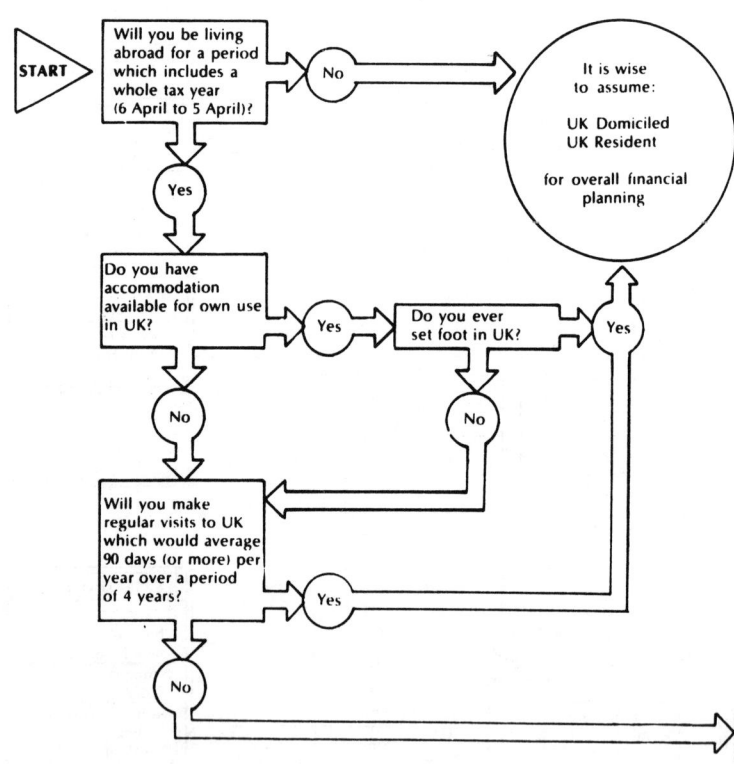

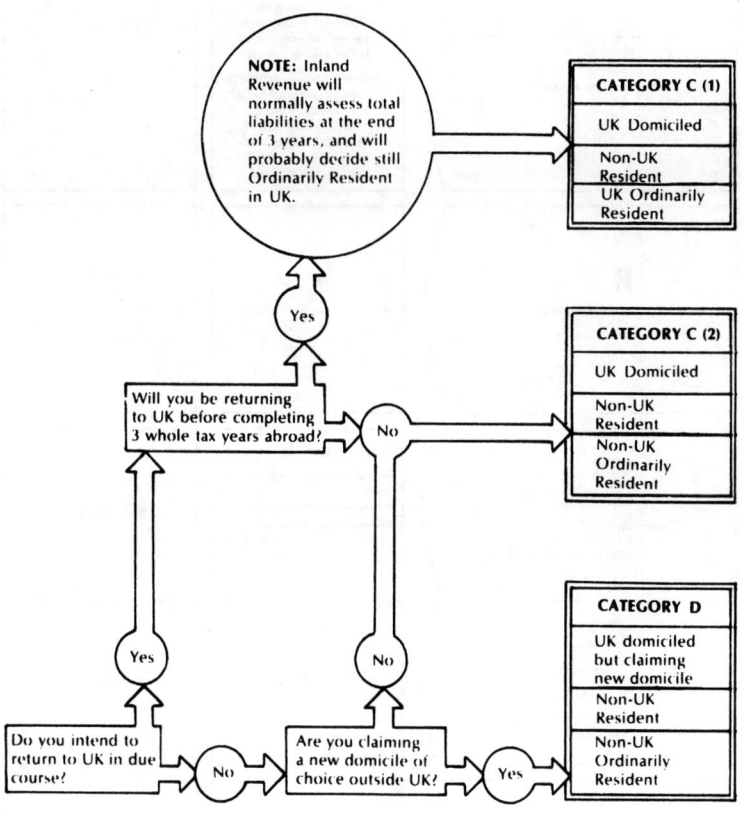

Client Category	UK Income Tax	
	Income arising in UK	Income arising Abroad
A Non-UK Domicile Non-UK Resident	• UK withholding tax deducted on dividends etc arising in UK • Overseas dividends collected in UK can be passed on gross of UK tax to non-residents • Some UK Government Stocks (exempt Gilts): interest and Bank and Building Society interest can be paid gross if non-UK ordinarily resident	No liability
B Non-UK Domicile UK Resident	Liable on all income arising in UK Able to claim normal UK Personal reliefs and exemptions	Liable on any income remitted to the UK (Income arising and retained outside UK is not assessed unless and until remitted to UK)
C1 UK Domicile Non-UK Resident UK Ordinarily Resident	As for Category A (but gilt exemptions do not apply while still ordinarily resident in UK also Bank and Building Society interest liable to deduction of CRT—composite rate tax not repayable	No liability
C2 UK Domicile Non-UK Resident Non-UK Ordinarily Resident	As for Category A	No liability
D Claiming Non-UK Domicile of Choice Non-UK Resident Non-UK Ordinarily Resident	As for Category A	No liability

UK Capital Gains Tax		UK Inheritance Tax	
Assets in UK	Assets Abroad	Assets in UK	Assets abroad
No liability (except perhaps on disposal of business property in UK CGTA. 1979 s 12)	No liability	Liability can arise on assets held in UK (Some Gilts exempt under IHTA 1984 s 602)	No liability (but may incur IHT liability if ever becomes 'deemed' UK domiciled)
Liable on gains realised in UK while UK resident and/or ordinarily resident	Liable on any Gain remitted to the UK (gains realised and retained outside UK are not assessed unless and until remitted to UK)	As for Category A	No liability (but may incur IHT liability in due course if 'deemed' UK domiciled)
Liable on Worldwide gains while still ordinarily UK Resident		Liable on Worldwide assets	
As for Category A			
As for Category A		Liable on Worldwide assets (if client successfully establishes a non-UK domicile of choice, liability will be as for Category A)	

Client Category	UK Taxation—effect on investments		
	UK Equities UK Loan Stocks UK Unit Trusts etc	UK exempt Government Stocks	Other UK Government Stocks (excluding exempt Gilts)
A Non-UK Domicile Non-UK Resident Not Ordinarily Resident in UK	(!) Beware IHT and UK withholding tax—although investment advantages may outweigh tax disadvantages	☺ Can claim interest gross of UK withholding tax, and asset is exempt from IHT	(!) Beware IHT and UK withholding tax—prefer UK Exempt Government Stocks if possible
B Non-UK Domicile UK Resident	(!) Beware IHT and CGT, plus: Income will be paid in UK net of withholding tax or CRT (composite rate tax) Prefer offshore alternatives, with income paid gross, and assets outside UK for CGT and IHT purposes		
C1 **UK Domicile** **Non-UK Resident** **UK Ordinarily Resident**	(!) Beware UK withholding tax—prefer offshore alternatives with less, or no, withholding taxes on income distribution (Offshore funds are usually cheaper to invest in than dealing directly with foreign markets)	(?) Strictly, cannot claim interest gross of UK withholding tax until no longer ordinarily UK resident (will receive any income net in interim)	(!) Beware UK withholding tax—prefer offshore alternatives with similar security : for example Allied Dunbar Sterling Fixed Interest Fund
C2 **UK Domicile** **Non-UK Resident** **Non-UK Ordinarily Resident**		☺ Can claim interest gross of UK withholding tax as not ordinarily UK resident (CARE if making claim to UK personal reliefs under TA 1988, s 278	
D Claiming Non-UK Domicile of Choice Non-UK Resident Non-UK Ordinarily Resident	(!) Apart from the tax disadvantage as described in C above the investment will form a UK connection which may damage the domicile claim prefer offshore alternatives	(?) If non-UK domicile is established, will be as for A above but in the interim a UK asset and a UK connection	(!) The same considerations apply as for UK equities for D prefer offshore alternatives eg Allied Dunbar Sterling Fixed Interest Fund

UK Taxation—effect on investments		UK Taxation—effect on money movement		
UK Bank and Building Society Deposits	**Joint holdings with spouse who is UK resident for tax purposes**	**Overseas Income remitted to UK**	**Capital Gains arising in UK**	**Overseas Capital Gains remitted to UK**
Can request Interest paid gross of CRT as UK non-resident—but Beware IHT	Could expose income and gains to UK tax liability	No tax implications to prevent free movement of money into UK (CARE if increasing UK assets—Beware IHT)		
	No immediate disadvantage while both UK resident	Will incur UK income tax if remitted to UK— Retain offshore	Delay realisation of any UK gains until after leaving UK if possible Gains realised while resident will incur CGT	Will incur CGT if remitted Retain offshore and only remit to limit of annual CGT exemption
Strictly, cannot claim interest gross of CRT until no longer ordinarily UK resident (will receive any income net in interim) Can claim interest gross of CRT as not ordinarily UK resident. Care if making claim to UK personal reliefs under TA 1988, s 278 —prefer offshore alternatives	Any assets held jointly with resident spouse are assessable to UK taxes. (each spouse should maintain separate bank account, investments and other assets in own sole name)	Remitting to UK will not incur a tax liability in itself— but it usually makes more practical sense to send all 'spare' income direct to offshore investment to save time, postage and paper	Will incur CGT liability if realised while still ordinarily UK resident—delay realisation until no longer UK ordinarily resident An ideal time to ensure that all UK gains already accrued are realised **do not delay** until after return to UK!	Will incur CGT liability if realised while still ordinarily resident **whether remitted to UK or not**— delay until not ordinarily resident An ideal time to realise gains but more practical to remit proceeds to offshore bank than to UK—**do not delay** until after return to UK!
UK Banking could be regarded as a strong remaining tie with UK and taken together with other UK links, invalidate non-domicile claim—**prefer offshore Bank Services**	Non-domicile claim would be rare if spouse remains in UK—joint assets with resident spouse would almost certainly defeat any non-UK domicile claim	Remittance of Income to UK may serve to reinforce UK links and increase UK assets	This would mark a disposal of UK assets and therefore severing of UK ties. Helpful in decreasing UK assets in event of non-domicile claim being successful	Remittance of capital to UK may serve to reinforce UK links and increase UK assets

4 Income arising in the United Kingdom

4.1 Introduction

In this and the following five chapters we look in more detail at the impact of UK taxes of various kinds on the British expatriate, and in the two subsequent chapters we describe some of the principles determining his liability to tax in another jurisdiction, particularly that of his overseas residence. The UK tax system is so complex that the use of the expression 'tax planning' indicates undue optimism in most individual cases. Nevertheless, to be forewarned is the only way to be forearmed in one's dealings with the tax administration in any country; and to act as far as possible in advance will in many cases save not only a great deal of time and trouble but considerable amounts of money as well.

Tax legislation is complex because it tries by means of general measures to apply equity to numberless individual instances. Anyone who deals professionally with the tax matters of expatriates soon becomes aware of the enormous variableness of their individual circumstances: in fact at times it seems that no two sets of circumstances are exactly alike. For this reason, if for no other, a Guide of this kind cannot provide all the answers. To obtain a complete picture, the expatriate must in any case consider any local taxation which applies in his country of residence and the provisions of any double taxation agreement between that country and the United Kingdom. But even when this has been done, in many cases the complications are such and the sums of money potentially involved so large that it is essential to seek individual professional advice.

For most British expatriates the source of their actual earnings will be outside the United Kingdom. But many will receive an income from one source or another in the United Kingdom itself. Many who were previously resident will already have investments in the United Kingdom, and many more will wish to invest there. It may also be the case that an expatriate will receive earnings from UK business or draw a pension from an earlier employment.

In any of these circumstances, a UK source of income will have a tax consequence, but the British tax system is such that the tax consequence may be different for every type of income. Earnings from employment are treated differently from pensions, which in turn are treated differently from business profits. Earned income is treated in a different manner from investment income, and different types of investment give rise to different methods of taxation.

This chapter looks in some detail at the taxation consequences attaching to the major types of income originating in the United Kingdom, so far as UK tax is concerned. Income from letting UK property is considered separately in Chapter 5, and further chapters deal with capital gains tax and inheritance tax.

4.2   The UK schedular system of income tax

An unusual feature of the UK income tax system is that different sources of income are assessed separately, with varying rules for computing the income, relief for losses, and due dates for payment of tax.

The tax schedules, as they are known, corresponding to each distinct source of income, originated in Addington's Act of 1803 which, by taxing each source separately with deduction of tax at source where possible, avoided the need for a return of total income. No UK taxpayer had to make such a return until Lloyd George introduced supertax on incomes over £3,000 in his 1909 'people's Budget'.

The sources of income covered by each of the schedules are broadly as follows:

Schedule A: rents from land
Schedule C: interest on government securities

Schedule D:
- Case I: profits from trades and businesses (self-employment)
- II: profits from professions and vocations (self-employment)
- III: interest on investments
- IV: interest on overseas securities
- V: income from overseas possessions
- VI: other annual profits or gains

Schedule E: income from employment and pension

Schedule F: income from dividends and distributions paid by UK companies and unit trusts

Schedule B: (annual value of commercial woodlands) was abolished in 1988.

A UK taxpayer with several sources of income may have to deal with several tax offices. As a general rule, Schedule E income is dealt with by the tax office for the area where the salary or pension is paid, and Schedule D Cases I and II profits are dealt with by the tax office covering the business address. Other income is dealt with by the tax office covering the taxpayer's home address if the taxpayer is UK resident.

4.3   Interest from bank and building society deposits

Income accruing to a UK deposit account is strictly speaking taxable in the United Kingdom under Schedule D, Case III.

However, where the beneficial owner of the account is not resident in the United Kingdom and certain other conditions are fulfilled, then under Extra-Statutory Concession B13 (1992) no action will be taken to pursue that tax charge on bank deposits or building society interest or from certificates of deposit, deep gain securities, or client account deposits.

The deduction of tax at source provisions on bank interest do not apply to a non-resident, provided that he has declared in writing to the deposit taker liable to pay interest that at the time of the declaration he is beneficially entitled to the interest and is not ordinarily resident in the United Kingdom. The declaration contains an undertaking that if the depositor becomes ordinarily resident in the United Kingdom he will notify the deposit taker accordingly and must be in the form prescribed by the Board of Inland Revenue and contain such information as they may reasonably require (TA 1988, ss 481(5)(*k*), 482(2)).

Where, exceptionally, a declaration does not incorporate the address of the person making it, it needs to be supported by a certificate from the deposit taker. In such a case, the deposit taker needs to certify that, to the best of his knowledge and belief, the persons to whom the declaration relates are not ordinarily resident in the United Kingdom; that the person making the declaration has undertaken to notify him of a relevant change in residence status; and that if he receives information indicating that any of the persons concerned are ordinarily resident in the United Kingdom, he will deduct tax. In addition the Revenue is empowered to prescribe or authorise the form of the declarations and certificates.

4.3.1 Extra-statutory concessions

The first condition attached to Concession B13 is that the individual concerned should be regarded as not resident in the United Kingdom for the whole of the year of assessment. This means that the concession is not available in either the year of departure or the year of return. Since the basis of assessment for established sources of income under Case III is the previous year basis, this means that the person leaving the United Kingdom in May 1991, for example, will be liable for tax on the accrued interest in 1992/93. In the normal course of events this tax would be payable in January 1993, but where a repayment claim (for tax deducted under PAYE prior to departure, perhaps) has been made, this tax will be set off against any repayment otherwise due.

The situation on returning to the United Kingdom is generally more serious, particularly if the deposit account has been inflated by extra savings during the period abroad. A person returning in July 1992 would be assessed on the interest arising in 1991/92, that is for a year during which he was non-resident. Another Extra-Statutory Concession (A11) which can be applied to some other sources of income briefly states that where liability is affected by the individual's residence then it will be computed with reference to the period of residence during the year of assessment. For example, someone becoming resident in the United Kingdom half way through the tax year will be taxed on only half the assessable income of the previous year if the preceding year basis is applicable (see also Chapter 12 — The returning expatriate). This concession is not granted in the case of UK bank interest.

The second condition in Concession B13 is that the non-resident should not be chargeable in the name of any trustee, agent or branch with the management and control of the interest.

Finally, if the interest is to be tax free the person must not make any claim to relief in respect of taxed income from UK sources (for example, a claim to personal allowances under TA 1988, s 278).

Joint accounts, where one party is resident and the other is non-resident, as is often the case with married expatriates, are wholly taxable (regardless of whether the account is with a UK bank or offshore) because the interest is generally not apportioned between the two individuals but accrues to them jointly and can be drawn by either of them. This is a point missed by many expatriates.

In general, UK bank and building society deposit accounts are to be avoided. If it is desired to maintain a deposit account with a British bank, it should be made with an offshore branch or subsidiary of the bank, for example, in the Isle of Man. In that way it will be beyond the reach of the UK legislation and attract no UK tax.

4.4   Interest from government, local authority and corporate stocks

Government stocks
In the main British government stocks are subject to UK income tax and the majority have tax deducted at source. But interest from certain stocks is exempt from tax if they are beneficially owned by a person not ordinarily resident in the United Kingdom. The stocks which are currently exempt are listed below.

10%	Treasury Loan 1993	9%	Treasury Loan 1994
12½%	Treasury Loan 1993	12¾%	Treasury Loan 1995
6%	Funding Loan 1993	9%	Treasury Loan 1992/96
13¾%	Treasury Loan 1993	15¼%	Treasury Loan 1996
14½%	Treasury Loan 1994	13¼%	Exchequer Loan 1996
10%	Treasury Loan 1994	13¾%	Treasury Loan 1997

$8\frac{3}{4}$%	Treasury Loan 1997	9%	Treasury Loan 2008
$6\frac{3}{4}$%	Treasury Loan 1995/98	9%	Conversion Stock 2011
$15\frac{1}{2}$%	Treasury Loan 1998	$5\frac{1}{2}$%	Treasury Loan 2008/12
$9\frac{1}{2}$%	Treasury Loan 1999	$7\frac{3}{4}$%	Treasury Loan 2012/15
9%	Conversion Stock 2000	$3\frac{1}{2}$%	War Loan 1952 or after
8%	Treasury Loan 2002/06	$2\frac{1}{2}$%	Index-linked Treasury
$8\frac{1}{2}$%	Treasury Loan 2007		Loan 2024

Since the majority of stocks suffer tax at source, the non-resident stockholder must apply for the gross payment of exempt stocks. Application should be made to The Inspector of Foreign Dividends, Lynwood Road, Thames Ditton, Surrey KT7 0DP.

Stocks normally paid without deduction of tax include $3\frac{1}{2}$ per cent War Loan and registered stocks and bonds on the National Savings Stock Register.

Exempt stocks have long been a mainstay for the appropriate portion of the British expatriate investor's portfolio because of their competitive yield and high security. They also form the basis of a large offshore gilt fund industry and both direct and fund investment can form part of a sound investment portfolio.

Local authority stocks
Interest from local authority stocks is generally paid after deduction of tax. The only exception to this is where the stock was issued for borrowing in a foreign currency. In that case, and subject to Treasury direction, the interest may be paid gross and be exempt from income tax if the stockholder is not resident in the United Kingdom.

Corporate stocks — debentures, etc
These, too, are generally paid effectively net of income tax at the basic rate, although arrangements can be made for interest to be paid gross under a double taxation agreement (see Chapter 11).

Any other interest
Subject to the exceptions described above and to the specific provisions of double taxation treaties (see below) all interest payments made to non-residents should be paid net of UK income tax at the basic rate.

Double taxation agreements
Where there is a double taxation treaty in force between the United Kingdom and the country of residence of the recipient,

then the treatment of interest may be covered therein. It is normal in these cases for interest to be payable gross and tax to be payable in the country of residence. Many agreements, however, have provision for a withholding tax in the country of origin. The appropriate agreement must be checked.

4.4.1 Dividends

Dividends paid by UK companies are technically paid gross, ie, there is no income tax deducted at source. However, alongside the dividend there is an associated tax credit currently equal to one-third of the net dividend. So far as the payer is concerned, this tax credit is accounted for and paid to the Inland Revenue as advance corporation tax (ACT). This ACT can be used to offset the payer's final or mainstream corporation tax liability in due course. So far as the payee is concerned the tax credit can be treated as analogous to income tax deducted at source. For the UK resident non-taxpayer, the credit can be repaid, and for the higher rate taxpayer, the quantum of dividend income on which tax will be calculated is the sum of the dividend plus tax credit.

Thus, where a person receives a dividend of £375, there will be a tax credit associated with the dividend of £125. For the non-taxpayer, this £125 can be repaid. If the recipient of the dividend had a marginal tax rate of 40 per cent, however, then there would be additional tax of £75 due on his dividend income:

Dividend	£375
Tax Credit	125
	£500
Tax @ 40%	200
Less: tax credit	125
Additional tax due	£75

This tax treatment applies to dividends and other distributions from UK companies, investment trusts, and unit trusts.

In general terms, the non-resident is not able to reclaim the tax credit. However, under certain double taxation agreements payment of the tax credit can be made subject to a UK withholding tax. This withholding tax is 15 per cent of the sum of the dividend plus tax credit, therefore allowing 40 per cent of the tax credit to be paid.

Where an expatriate is entitled to personal allowances under TA 1988, s 278 then the tax credit can be repaid up to the amount of allowances due: see **4.15**.

4.5 Life assurance policies

The benefits payable under UK Life Assurance Policies are liable to UK tax for non-residents and residents alike. For tax purposes, policies are classified as 'qualifying' or 'non-qualifying'. A qualifying policy must be held for ten years, or three-quarters of the original term agreed, and the premiums must be paid regularly, at least once a year, and must be spread evenly throughout the duration of the policy. For a qualifying policy normally there will be no tax liability where the proceeds are payable to the original policyholder or to somebody to whom the policy has been given. In the case of a non-qualifying policy, tax may be payable on the proceeds. (For a single premium bond, for example, the permitted annual withdrawal is a cumulative 5 per cent per annum, which, if taken, could be for a maximum period of up to 20 years.) Tax is payable only by higher rate taxpayers — which includes those who are moved into the higher rate when any gain on total surrender or excess withdrawal is added to their annual taxable income — and is charged at the difference between the basic and the higher rate of tax (15 per cent for the 1992/93 tax year). For non-UK residents without other significant amounts of UK income, this will generally mean that there is no tax due.

It is important to bear in mind though, that this seemingly beneficial tax treatment is granted to take into account the tax that is paid by UK Life Assurance Companies on the profits and gains within policy funds. Currently, franked income (that from UK equities and gilt edged securities) is taxed at 25 per cent, all other income (from foreign equities and Eurobonds, for example) and capital gains are taxed at 33 per cent but of course the allowance available to individuals to offset the first of £5,800 of gain, is not applicable. For non-UK residents 'offshore policies' may prove to be a better investment. An 'offshore policy' is one issued by a life assurance company resident in a tax-haven where policy funds pay little or no tax on income and gains and the policy proceeds are similarly free of tax.

Expatriates returning to the United Kingdom should note that the proceeds of policies effected after 17 November 1983 may be fully liable to tax on the accrued profits, ie without the benefit of the basic rate tax credit, although the profit will be apportioned in direct relation to the periods of residence and non-residence during the policy term and only that portion relating to the period of UK residence will be subject to tax. (The proceeds of offshore policies taken out before 18 November 1983 continue to be free of liability to UK taxation.)

These comments refer only to UK taxation and non-UK residents must also take account of any local tax liability that may be due on policy proceeds.

Where life assurance premium relief is available (for a qualifying policy issued on or before 13 March 1984) the premiums may be paid net of the relief — currently 12½ per cent of the premium. The policyholder is eligible for relief if the policy is written on his life or that of his spouse, if either of them pays the premiums, and if the person paying is resident in the United Kingdom for tax purposes. Where the policyholder and his spouse will both be non-resident for the whole of a tax year the premiums must be paid gross, but net payments may be resumed when they again take up UK residence.

4.6 National Savings

Most of the investments offered by the Department for National Savings are tax-free both for residents and non-residents. But the yield from these investments largely reflects this, in that greater yields can often be obtained elsewhere. As with other 'tax-free' investments there is no guarantee that the proceeds will remain so overseas.

The main taxable National Savings investments are the National Savings Bank investment account, income bonds and capital bonds which usually offer very competitive interest returns. Interest on all of these is always paid without deduction of income tax.

4.7 Pensions

Many expatriates will, whether now or later, receive pension income from the United Kingdom and for tax purposes this income may be divided into three separate groups:

(1) State pensions — these include Old Age Pension and the State Earnings Related Pension Scheme.
(2) Private pensions — such as an occupational pension payable by a UK employer or self-employed and personal pensions (including Personal Pension Plans which became available from 1 July 1988).
(3) Government pensions — pensions arising from UK government service: eg an armed services pension, an NHS pension, a teacher's pension etc.

State pensions are always paid gross and can be paid in any country. The pensioner is liable for tax in the country where he is resident, but where he receives any other pension taxable in the United Kingdom (see below), the State Retirement Pension will usually be taxed alongside that other pension. This is carried out either by a reduction of allowances or by the use of the higher rate of taxation in addition to the basic rate.

Private pensions continue to be liable to tax in the United Kingdom — they are likely also to be liable for tax in the country in which the expatriate is resident. Fortunately the United Kingdom has double taxation treaties with more than 90 countries, including those where expatriate Britons are most commonly to be found. Most of these treaties include an article covering private pensions and provide for the pension to be paid gross in the United Kingdom and taxable only in the country of residence.

Government pensions are always taxable in the United Kingdom and, like private pensions, they are likely also to be liable for tax in the country of residence. Once again, relief is available where there is a double taxation agreement in force — this will normally provide for government pensions to be taxable only in the United Kingdom. (More information on double taxation agreements may be found in Chapter 11.)

Non-residents in receipt of a UK pension will often qualify for UK personal allowances (TA 1988, s 278) and these allowances should be claimed.

4.8 Employments

The taxation treatment of employments which are carried on partly within and partly outside the United Kingdom is fully described in Chapter 2. Some non-residents do, however, have employments which are carried on wholly in the United Kingdom. Commonly, these are directorships where the non-resident does not work full-time in the employment but attends board meetings, etc, in the United Kingdom. The whole of the remuneration from an entirely domestic employment is liable to UK income tax. Taxable too are benefits in kind and travelling expenses from the overseas home to the United Kingdom received or incurred in the performance of such employments, unless they are wholly, exclusively and necessarily incurred in the performance of the duties; TA 1988, s 198, *Taylor v Provan* [1974] STC 168.

Where a non-UK domiciled individual comes to work in the United Kingdom and was not resident in the United Kingdom during either of the two preceding tax years or was not present in the United Kingdom at any time during the two years up to the date of his arrival, he is entitled to relief for travel between the United Kingdom and his normal place of abode abroad for a period of five years, so long as the cost is borne or reimbursed by the employer. The journey includes travel from the home in the United Kingdom to the home overseas. Where the employee is in the United Kingdom for a continuous period of 60 days or more, he is entitled to relief for two visits a year by his spouse and minor children so long as the expenses are paid for or reimbursed by the employer. Apportionment is possible in cases of duality of purpose. There are provisions to prevent double allowances.

Where it can be shown that some part of the duties of the employment are carried out overseas then part of the remuneration should be exempt from tax.

4.9   Trades and professions

Where a non-resident has trading income arising in the United Kingdom this will normally be liable to UK income tax. It is important, however, to consider the nature of the trade, where it is actually carried on, and whether or not an agent is involved.

A trade *with* the United Kingdom should not be confused with a trade *within* the United Kingdom. The latter is certainly taxable but the former may not be. A non-resident trader may have a representative office or an advertising department within the United Kingdom, he may even have a sales agent in the United Kingdom, without incurring any income tax liability (*Grainger v Gough* (1896) 3 TC 311; *Smith & Co v Greenwood* (1922) 8 TC

193). But care must be taken with agents, as discussed below. An advertising or representative office will not be trading in the United Kingdom if, for example, the contracts for the sale of goods, or for services, are in fact made overseas directly with the trader. This would constitute trading *with* the United Kingdom. But if the overseas trade was represented by a UK sales office, for example, where orders were taken and paid for locally, then this would constitute trading *within* the United Kingdom.

In the simple cases of sale of goods and services, the position is fairly clear cut, but if the trade involves both manufacturing and selling in different countries then the situation becomes more complex. Where only selling takes place in the United Kingdom, the profit assessed may be limited to the merchanting profit under The Taxes Management Act 1970 (TMA 1970), s 81. Where UK branch profits do not appear to show the true profit, a proportion of the total worldwide profit may be charged in the United Kingdom based on the turnover in the United Kingdom, under TMA 1970, s 80. Such a situation allows for tax avoidance by arranging for profits to be realised in the least onerous fiscal regime. Needless to say, this is counteracted by anti-avoidance legislation such as the transfer pricing rules contained in TA 1988, ss 770–773.

Where a non-resident trades within the United Kingdom he will be liable to tax, but collecting that tax is another matter, given that courts will not normally enforce foreign tax debts. TMA 1970, ss 78 and 79 attempt to get around this by providing that a non-resident trading in the United Kingdom will be chargeable in the name of any branch or agent in the United Kingdom. Thus the UK sales office mentioned above would be a taxable or chargeable entity in that case. The only exception to this is where the agent is an independent broker or general commission agent carrying on a *bona fide* brokerage or commission agency.

4.10 Royalties and patents

Copyright and UK patent royalties paid to non-residents normally have income tax deducted at source by the payer (see, however, Chapter 11). The payer is assessable even if he fails to deduct the tax. The sale of a patent in the United Kingdom by a non-resident vendor involves the deduction of basic rate tax by the purchaser from the consideration paid, under TA 1988, s 524(3).

Where copyright royalties are paid through a third party that party may be liable on the net sum, ie the royalty less commission, TA 1988, s 536(3), (4).

4.11   Maintenance payments

Maintenance payments under a pre-15 March 1988 UK court order were, until 5 April 1989, paid subject to deduction of tax at source unless within the small payment limits of TA 1988, s 351.

For payments after 5 April 1989 under pre-15 March 1988 arrangements:

(1)   the payer gets tax relief on payments up to the level for which he got relief for 1988/89; and

(2)   an amount equal to that received in 1988/89 is treated as part of the recipient's total income;

(3)   however, the difference between the married person's allowance and the single person's allowance (for the relevant year of assessment) is exempt from tax in the recipient's hands.

All payments of maintenance are paid gross — without tax deducted by the payer.

Payers under the old rules may, if they prefer, switch to the current rules mentioned below. These rules will then apply to the recipient as well. An election, which will apply for a whole tax year, can be made at any time during the year and up to 12 months after. An election may be beneficial if payments increase, and the limit for relief 'pegged' at the 1988/89 level is below the maximum amount of relief available under the new rules.

For court orders and maintenance agreements made on or after 15 March 1988:

(1)   the recipient is not liable to tax on any payments received;

(2)   where one divorced or separated spouse is required to make payments to the other, the payer qualifies for tax relief (at basic and higher rates) for payments up to a limit equal to the difference between the single and married person's allowances (£1,720 for 1992/93) until the recipient remarries;

(3)   there is no tax relief for other new maintenance or alimony payments;

(4)   payments are made gross (ie without deduction of tax).

4.12 Trust and estate income

Tax on income received by a non-resident from an estate in the course of administration in the United Kingdom is initially charged on income distributed in the year of receipt and ultimately the total income is reallocated over the administration period on a day to day basis unless he has an absolute interest in the residue, or a share of it (TA 1988, s 695). The personal representatives will deduct tax at the basic rate and issue a tax certificate on form R185-E for the tax deducted. The income is then treated in the same way as any other UK-taxed income and a repayment claim may be made or a higher rate liability may arise.

Where the non-resident has an absolute interest in residue the income is again subject to basic rate tax being withheld by the personal representatives but in this case the income under TA 1988, s 696 is allocated on an arising basis and not on a day to day apportionment over the whole administration period. Relief from higher rate tax is available where IHT has been paid on accrued income at the date of death (TA 1988, s 699).

In the case of trust income a life tenant of a UK trust would receive income subject to tax at the basic rate, whereas the beneficiary of a discretionary UK trust would receive his share of income less UK tax at both the basic rate and an additional 10 per cent surcharge, ie currently 35 per cent, under TA 1988, s 687. Again, any overpayment of UK tax may be recovered and any underpayment of higher rate liability remains payable.

4.13 Avoidance of higher rate liability

Where UK investment income is sufficient, the non-resident may find that he has an individual liability to higher rate taxation in addition to any basic rate tax that may have been withheld at source. In many cases the tax charge can be limited to the basic rate by transferring investments to an overseas holding company in an appropriate tax haven. For example, if investments were held by an investment company in the Isle of Man with directors in, say, Hong Kong, it would be a non-resident company subject, in the Isle of Man, to a flat rate of tax of only £500. As a non-resident company, the liability to tax on its UK investment income would be limited under TA 1988, s 1 to basic rate only.

Despite the obvious attractions, expatriates considering this route should first indulge in some careful consideration. The costs involved in establishing and running an offshore company can be sizeable and nowadays the savings to be made are much less than in previous years, the maximum saving is now 15 per cent. Transferring the ownership of assets into an offshore company can also be a costly business especially where there is stamp duty to be taken into account: share transfers are charged at $\frac{1}{2}$ per cent and conveyances of land and buildings are charged at 1 per cent.

Where it is calculated that the tax saving is likely to outweigh the costs involved, there are still a couple of factors to be borne in mind before proceeding. First, in view of the anti-avoidance provisions of TA 1988, s 739 the offshore investment company route should only be considered by individuals not ordinarily resident in the United Kingdom and the company should be wound up before UK residence is resumed.

This means that the procedure is only suitable as a means of tax limitation for the long-term non-resident.

Secondly, however, care is required because, as in all tax matters, if there is first, a pre-ordained series of transactions and steps inserted which have no business purpose apart from avoidance of tax, the inserted steps will be ignored for tax purposes: see *Craven v White*, [1988] STC 476.

4.14 Lloyd's Underwriters

The taxation of Lloyd's Underwriters is a specialist subject and the comments here are confined to areas of particular interest to non-resident names.

Lloyd's income arises in the United Kingdom and is classified as a trade carried on in the United Kingdom subject to UK tax. It is normally desirable for Lloyd's deposits to be arranged by way of letter of credit or bank guarantee as, for example, exempt gilts held as part of Lloyd's deposits or reserves remain UK taxable as connected with a business carried on in the United Kingdom (*Owen v Sassoon* [1950] 32 TC 101) (apart from $3\frac{1}{2}$ per cent War Loan). The CGT and IHT exemptions however continue to apply.

The basis of assessment for Lloyd's investment income may not be followed by the overseas Revenue which might, for example, assess the investment income as it arises even though it is not distributed until the account is closed. United States tax paid which would be refunded to a UK resident is treated as an expense so far as a non-resident is concerned and merely reduces the gross income. Transfers to a special reserve fund would not normally have any effect for foreign tax purposes, although they would affect the UK tax payable and therefore the amount available for credit. Where the UK tax is fully relieved overseas there is no advantage in a transfer to the special reserve fund, although care has to be taken to ensure that foreign tax credits are not inadvertently lost.

There are special rules in certain countries for Lloyd's Names, in particular the United States and Canada.

4.15 Non-resident's entitlement to UK personal allowances

Certain classes of non-residents may obtain relief against UK assessable income through entitlement to the normal personal allowances under TA 1988, s 278.

The classes of individuals to which the relief applies include the following:

(1) Commonwealth citizens and citizens of the Republic of Ireland;
(2) persons who are or who have been in the service of the Crown;
(3) missionaries;
(4) servants of British Protectorates;
(5) residents of the Isle of Man or Channel Islands;
(6) persons abroad for health reasons after residence in the United Kingdom;
(7) widows of Crown servants;
(8) residents of countries where relief is given under a double taxation treaty.

In addition, double taxation agreements with many countries provide that the relief applies to residents of that country.

This tax relief is useful where the non-resident has a significant income taxable in the United Kingdom. Where the UK income is small, it may not be worth the trouble of claiming on an annual basis but possibly every few years (the time limit for the claim is six years).

5 Tax aspects of UK property

Peter Goodman MA, FCA ATII, of Wilkins Kennedy

Expatriates often retain property in the United Kingdom which is let during the period of absence overseas. The retention of such property ensures that the expatriate has a place to live in the United Kingdom on the completion of his overseas work, and may be a protection against rises in house prices during the period of absence.

Before entering into letting arrangements, the expatriate needs to give careful consideration to the proposed tenancy arrangements, with particular attention being given to rights of possession. Standard tenancy arrangements may create difficulties at a future date, and consequently advice should be sought from experienced professional advisers in relation to UK landlord and tenant law.

5.1 Rental income

Taxation matters in connection with lettings also need careful review. Income from UK property, being income arising from a source in the United Kingdom, is chargeable to UK tax at basic and, where applicable, higher rates. Assessment to tax is under either Schedule A (Unfurnished Lettings) or Schedule D, Case VI (Furnished Lettings). Expatriates resident in a country which has a double tax treaty with the United Kingdom will find that it is normally the case that the treaty provides for rental income to be taxed by the country in which the property is situated.

In preparing the statement of letting income for Inland Revenue purposes it is useful to give details of the property address, the UK letting agents, and in whose beneficial ownership the property vests. These details will assist the Inland Revenue in accurately assessing the income source. The statement should show gross income receivable less allowable expenses paid in respect of the letting incurred during the period covered by the statement. Expenses associated with the letting may include:

(1) water rates;
(2) agents' commission;
(3) building and contents insurance, and valuation fees for insurance purposes;
(4) service charges for equipment;
(5) repairs and maintenance (but not capital expenditure, eg central heating/double glazing installation);
(6) ground rent;
(7) professional charges for preparing the letting statement;
(8) advertising;
(9) wear and tear allowance (for furnished lettings only — being 10 per cent of gross rent receivable less rates paid by the landlord: Inland Revenue Press Release, 13 October 1977);
(10) cleaning;
(11) garden upkeep;
(12) inventory check-in/check-out costs;
(13) tenancy agreement charges.

Mortgage loan interest is not an allowable expense in arriving at net rental income, but may be allowed as a deduction in arriving at assessable letting income. Overdraft interest is not an allowable expense or deduction for tax purposes. A loan taken to replace an overdraft used to finance property acquisition or improvement will generally not qualify for tax relief (*Lawson (Inspector of Taxes) v Brooks* [1992] STC 76).

In order to obtain tax relief on interest, a number of conditions need to be met. The interest must be in respect of a loan to acquire or improve property and must be payable in the United Kingdom on an advance from a bank carrying on a *bona fide* banking business in the United Kingdom, or it must be annual interest chargeable to tax under Schedule D, Case III. It is prudent for the loan to be taken out in the United Kingdom from a UK bank or other lender, but it is understood that a loan arranged through the UK branch of a recognised overseas bank will be acceptable. Additionally, the property in the United Kingdom must be let at a commercial rent for at least 26 weeks in a 52-week period, and when not so let must be either available for letting at such a rent or undergoing works of construction or repair. Lettings at below the market rate, taking into account maintenance and repairing liabilities, result in loan interest relief being disallowed.

Qualifying interest in excess of net rental income from a property may be set off against other UK rental income. Any unrelieved balance may be carried forward to be deducted against rental income arising in the next year, provided that the property continues to be let at a full commercial rent.

Special rules apply if the loan is within the mortgage interest relief at source system (MIRAS), and this is dealt with at **5.5**.

The statement of letting income is normally prepared and submitted to the Inland Revenue by the property owner(s) direct or by their taxation agents. To ensure that the letting income is taxed at the correct rate, details of other UK source income received in the tax year should be provided. Additionally, personal allowances should be specifically claimed.

5.2   Relief for letting furnished rooms

New rules introduced by F(No 2)A 1992, Sched 10, provide tax relief for 1992/93 and future years, up to a limit of £3,250, to individuals, both owner-occupiers and tenants, who receive income from the letting of furnished rooms in their only or main residence. The relief is only available where income from furnished lettings is chargeable to tax under Schedule D, Case VI or Schedule D, Case 1 (a trade). Gross annual rents from this sort of letting which do not exceed £3,250 are exempt from tax. The limit is halved in the case of joint ownership of a property, although married couples will be able to arrange for the income, and the allowance, to belong to either one of them or to both of them as they prefer.

5.3   Administration and collection of tax

This is a complex area which can create a great deal of confusion for the expatriate. Where rents are paid direct by the tenant to the expatriate whose usual place of abode is outside the United Kingdom, then basic rate tax must be deducted from gross rents and paid to the Inland Revenue by the tenant (TA 1988, s 43). Payment of rent into a UK bank account held by the expatriate does not avoid the obligation of the tenant to deduct tax at source. It is important to note that, even if basic rate tax has been deducted by the tenant in these circumstances, it is still necessary to provide the Inland Revenue with a statement of rental income for each tax year in order that the correct income tax liability can be calculated.

Where the property is let through an agent, the provisions of TMA 1970, s 78 apply. This provides that the non-resident owner is assessed and charged to income tax in the name of the agent in the same manner as the non-resident person would have been assessed and charged had he been resident in the United Kingdom. The practical effect of this is that the Inland Revenue assesses the agent on the net rental income of the expatriate and the agent then discharges the income tax liability. There is no legal obligation on the agent therefore to deduct basic rate tax at source from rents remitted to the expatriate but, given the agent's responsibilities laid down in TMA 1970, s 78, the agent will ensure that sufficient tax is withheld from rents to satisfy the expected tax liability. A statutory right of indemnity from the tenant in respect of tax charged (not interest or penalties which may arise from late payment of tax or failure to make the necessary returns) is contained within TMA 1970, s 83(2). In the event that the agent has made an excessive retention in relation to the tax liability arising, such retention should be repaid to the expatriate once the lettings statement and liability to tax have been agreed with the Inland Revenue.

The agent may, in the interim, place the tax reserve in a gross interest yielding account. Gross bank deposit interest is normally not taxable on the expatriate by virtue of Extra-Statutory Concession B13, provided the appropriate certificate of non-residence is signed and the expatriate is not assessable in the name of an agent in the United Kingdom. The presence of a letting agent will not generally prevent the application of the concession, provided that the interest arising is beneficially owned by the expatriate, the deposit is not excessive in relation to rent arising, and the agent's authority is restricted to the withdrawal of funds solely for the purpose of discharging the income tax liability arising on the rents.

Tax on lettings income is normally payable on 1 January in the year of assessment.

5.4 Furnished holiday lettings

Letting furnished property as holiday accommodation within the terms of the legislation may secure a beneficial tax treatment of expatriates with other UK source income. Furnished holiday lettings are treated as a trade if the following conditions are met:

(1) the accommodation must be in the United Kingdom and let furnished on a commercial basis with a reasonable expectation of making a profit;
(2) it must be available for letting to the public at large for at least 140 days in any tax year;
(3) actual lettings must be at least 70 days in the tax year (although in the first and last years in which the trade is carried on the rules are modified);
(4) in a seven-month period, including the months that the property is let, no single let should normally be longer than 31 days.

The main income tax benefits to derive from the treatment of the activity as a trade relate to the ability to relieve losses against other UK income and the payment of tax in two instalments. There is no change to the administration and collection of income tax as described above. For CGT purposes the expatriate may, in certain circumstances, and especially if a spouse remains resident and has an interest in the property, derive a benefit from the availability of roll-over relief and retirement relief relating to business assets.

5.5 Mortgage interest relief at source (MIRAS)

MIRAS was introduced in April 1983, enabling UK interest payments to be made net of the basic rate of income tax to qualifying lenders. The loan on which interest payments arise must have been taken out for the purchase (or improvement, before 6 April 1988) of a property in the United Kingdom which is used wholly or to a substantial extent as the only or main residence of the borrower, his spouse (or before April 1988 a dependent relative or a former or separated spouse). MIRAS applies only to the first £30,000 of a loan which satisfies these conditions, and expatriates are not, as a class, excluded from MIRAS relief. Qualifying lenders include most UK building societies, banks, insurance companies and specialised mortgage funding schemes.

An expatriate working full-time overseas may be unable to satisfy the condition that any UK property retained is used 'wholly or to a substantial extent' as his only or main residence. 'Substantial' is not defined in the tax legislation, but it is understood that the Inland Revenue regards this as six months or more in the year. If the expatriate's spouse and family continue to live in the UK property then the condition may be satisfied. Additionally, Extra-Statutory

Concession A27 allows temporary absences of up to a year to be ignored in determining whether a property is used as an only or main residence.

In the event that the above conditions cannot be satisfied, MIRAS relief may continue by the application of Extra-Statutory Concession A27. This principally applies when a person is required by reason of his employment to move from his home to another place overseas for a period not expected to exceed four years. MIRAS will continue to apply to mortgage interest payments in respect of a loan for the purchase of a property used as an only or main residence before working overseas, provided this property can reasonably be expected to be used again as such on his return. Relief is not given beyond a period of four years, but if there is a further temporary absence after the property has been re-occupied for a minimum period of three months, the four-year test will apply to the new absence without regard to the previous absence. It should be noted that if arrangements are entered into to take advantage of the concession for tax avoidance purposes, it is likely that the Inland Revenue will deny the application of the concession (*R v IRC, ex p Fulford Dobson* [1987] STC 344).

If an expatriate on an overseas tour of duty purchases a property in the United Kingdom in the course of a leave period, and uses that property as an only or main residence for a period of not less than three months before his return to the place of his overseas employment, he will be regarded as satisfying the condition that the property was being used as his only or main residence before he went away, and MIRAS will be applied.

Where a loan continues within MIRAS and the benefit of Extra-Statutory Concession A27 is claimed, the legislation does not expressly provide relief for interest paid over £30,000 against letting income. Once the loan is taken out of MIRAS, interest relief is available without restriction against rental income provided the conditions mentioned earlier (at **5.1**) are satisfied. Generally the Inland Revenue does not apply the rules strictly so that MIRAS is received on the first £30,000 of the loan, with interest paid on the loan in excess of this being relieved against rental income.

This relaxation of the rules by the Inland Revenue may change, and is not embodied in law or extra-statutory concession. It is therefore advisable to consider, on the commencement of the letting, the manner in which tax relief for loan interest is to be obtained. Loans substantially in excess of £30,000 on property commercially let should be withdrawn from MIRAS, thereby securing a full deduction for interest paid without reliance on Inland Revenue practice.

Mortgage interest relief is administered by the Central Unit (MIRAS) 1st Floor, St Johns House, Merton Road, Bootle, L69 4EJ.

5.6   Capital gains tax: principal private residence

The disposal of UK property by an expatriate during a tax year throughout which he is not resident and not ordinarily resident for UK tax purposes does not give rise to a charge to CGT.

For the tax year of return to the United Kingdom, Extra-Statutory Concession D2 provides that 'a person who is treated as resident in the United Kingdom for any year of assessment from the date of his arrival here but who has not been regarded at any time during the period of 36 months immediately preceding the date of his arrival as resident or ordinarily resident here, is charged to CGT only in respect of the chargeable gains accruing to him from disposals made after his arrival in the United Kingdom'. However, extra-statutory concessions will not be given in any case where an attempt is made to use them for tax avoidance, and after the judgment in *R v IRC, ex p Fulford Dobson* (1987) care should be taken in respect of any transaction involving a chargeable gain undertaken in the period 5 April to the date of arrival in the United Kingdom.

Expatriates who retain their home in the United Kingdom during their period of absence overseas should carefully consider the conditions to be satisfied after returning to the United Kingdom for exemption from CGT on a subsequent sale. These conditions are as follows:

(1)   The property must be the individual's only or main residence throughout the period of ownership except for all or any part of the last 36 months of ownership (24 months for disposals before 19 March 1991). If the property has been an only or main residence for part of the period of ownership the gain is apportioned between the exempt and non-exempt periods.

(2)   The exemption applies to dwelling houses and land comprising garden and ground which are for the occupation and

enjoyment of the main residence up to the permitted area. The permitted area is defined as 0.5 of a hectare, being approximately 1.25 acres (inclusive of the site of the dwelling house), although in any particular case the permitted area may be a larger area as the 'Commissioners may determine, if satisfied that regard being had to the size and the character of the dwelling house, that larger area is required for the reasonable enjoyment of it as a residence'. (TCGA 1992, s 222(3).)

(3) Certain periods of absence from the dwelling are treated as periods of residence provided the dwelling house was the only property eligible for relief and was occupied as such both before and after the periods of absence. These periods which can be used on a cumulative basis are:

    (a) any period or periods of absence which do not in total exceed three years; and

    (b) any period of absence throughout which the individual worked in an employment or office all the duties of which were performed outside the United Kingdom; and

    (c) any period or periods of absence not exceeding four years in total throughout which the individual was prevented from residing in the dwelling house in consequence of the situation of his place of work or because his employer required him to live elsewhere so that his duties of employment could be effectively carried out.

Expatriates need to pay close attention to condition (b). It is clear that all duties of employment must be performed outside the United Kingdom. This is in contrast to income tax rules where incidental duties performed in the United Kingdom may be disregarded under the provisions of TA 1988, s 335. The performance of such incidental UK duties could inadvertently jeopardise the CGT relief. The condition is also framed in terms of employment or office and does not cover self-employment.

The requirements as to occupation of the property both before and after the period of absence are of considerable significance. If the expatriate returns to the United Kingdom and does not occupy his former main residence because he owns another property, then a chargeable gain may arise on disposal. Extra-Statutory Concession D4 provides assistance to the expatriate where he is unable to resume residence in his previous home because the terms of his employment require him to work elsewhere. The concession deems the condition of re-occupation after the period of absence to be satisfied.

Where an expatriate has sold his UK home during his overseas absence and purchased another property which is to be occupied on his return to the United Kingdom the gain attributable to the period of time from purchase to actual occupation may be chargeable to CGT on disposal. This arises if the property has not been occupied as the main or only property on purchase, even though it replaces a former main residence occupied as such, before leaving the United Kingdom. Such transactions can present an unfortunate tax pitfall for the expatriate, although the legislation contains specific relief for expatriates who live in job-related accommodation overseas. This is defined as where it is necessary for the proper performance of the duties of the employment that the employee should reside in that accommodation.

Another point to consider carefully is that for the principal private residence exemption to apply, the expatriate must have no other property eligible for CGT exemption as an only or main residence throughout the period of absence. This creates a difficulty as the expatriate may have an interest in an overseas residence — either by way of ownership or rental — which will be a residence eligible for relief. In these circumstances the expatriate should consider submitting to the Inland Revenue an election under TCGA 1992, s 222(5) that the UK property is the expatriate's only or main residence to satisfy the statutory requirements. There is a two-year time limit from acquisition of the interest in the additional property to make the election.

If part of the gain on a principal private residence is in charge to CGT and the property has been wholly or partly let as residential accommodation during the period of ownership a further relief is available. The relief is the lesser of £40,000 (£20,000 for disposals before 19 March 1991) and the gain otherwise exempt under the general rules referred to as (1)–(3) above.

5.7   Inheritance tax

Non-resident, UK-domiciled individuals remain liable to IHT on their worldwide estate. A UK will should specifically cover the disposition of all UK properties.

6 Capital gains tax

6.1 Residence

The Taxation of Chargeable Gains Act 1992 (TCGA 1992), s 2 provides that an individual resident or ordinarily resident in the United Kingdom is subject to CGT on his worldwide capital gains. In order, therefore, to avoid UK CGT it is essential to cease to be normally resident in the United Kingdom. This normally requires three complete tax years of non-residence or, when the individual concerned is in full-time employment overseas, one complete tax year of non-residence. Exemption from CGT then normally applies to gains accruing to the individual from disposals made after the date of his departure (ie he does not have to wait for a new tax year, or for a full tax year to elapse: Extra-Statutory Concession D2, 1992). The liability to CGT of an expatriate returning to the United Kingdom is discussed in detail in Chapter 12.

6.2 Husband and wife

The residence statuses of a husband and wife are determined independently. Despite this, the CGT exemption for assets transferred between spouses married and living together is nonetheless preserved. In *Gubay v Kington* [1984] STC 499, it was held that the transfer of a chargeable asset by a UK resident spouse to a non-resident spouse was not a chargeable event. The scope for transferring an asset from a resident to a non-ordinarily resident spouse before sale to avoid CGT is limited as was illustrated in *R v IRC ex p Fulford Dobson* [1987] STC 344. In this case a wife transferred a farm to her husband who went to work in Germany and the farm was sold four days after his departure. The Revenue's refusal to apply Extra-Statutory Concession D2 (1992), because an attempt had been made to use it for tax avoidance, was upheld.

6.3   Emigration

A person emigrating from the United Kingdom would normally leave the disposal of his assets showing capital gains until after his departure (taking due account of his liability in the new jurisdiction). The disposal should be deferred until after the following 5 April because the Revenue is likely to refuse to apply Extra-Statutory Concession D2 (1992). Investments showing losses would normally be sold before the date of departure in order to crystallise a loss which might be of use on any future return to the United Kingdom.

If the assets in question are used in, or in connection with, a business, there are further important considerations. See **6.5**.

6.4   Property

Although non-residents may be exempt from CGT in respect of a disposal of most investments, it is necessary to look rather more carefully in the case of land and buildings. Section 776 of TA 1988, provides that a capital profit from dealing or developing land directly or indirectly is assessed to tax under Schedule D, Case VI as UK income irrespective of the residence of the owner. Section 777(9) of TA 1988 enables the Board to direct that basic rate income tax may be withheld from the sale proceeds, although in practice this has proved ineffective in many cases, as the Revenue have not been aware of the disposal until too late to raise the necessary direction and the non-resident has received the sale proceeds gross. Section 776 does not apply to private residences exempt from CGT as a main residence.

6.5   Business gains

6.5.1   Sale of a business

A not uncommon spur to emigration occurs where a person resident or ordinarily resident in the United Kingdom is intending to dispose of his business, consisting either of shares in a company or the goodwill of an unincorporated business. This gives rise to a number of problems. Although under Extra-Statutory Concession D2 a person emigrating from the United Kingdom is *normally* regarded as neither resident nor ordinarily resident from the day following the day of departure this is a purely concessional treatment as, at law, a person resident for part of the tax year is resident for the entire tax year. The Revenue is likely to refuse to apply the concession so the contract for the disposal of the shares or business should be deferred until after the following 5 April. Even then the problems are not necessarily over as the Revenue or the courts might infer a prior oral contract, or prior agreement sufficient to constitute a contract, where all the terms and conditions of the sale were finalised before final sale. In this connection there is precedent for holding that correspondence between the parties before the final contract can create a binding contract (*J H & S Timber Ltd v Quirk* [1973] STC 111) and that the beneficial ownership can pass before any transfer of legal title (*Ayerst v C & K (Construction) Ltd* [1975] STC 345, *Wood Preservation Ltd v Prior* [1968] 45 TC 112). Gains in the year of departure would also be outside Extra-Statutory Concession D2 if the business was carried on in the United Kingdom through a branch or agency (press release of 6 April 1989, amending ESC D2).

Section 28 of TCGA 1992 states that the date of disposal for CGT is the time the contract was made, and if the contract is conditional it is the time when the condition is satisfied. It would, however, be hazardous to enter into arrangements designed specifically to postpone the date of disposal in order to allow time for emigration, as this might give rise to a series of transactions or a single composite transaction, the effect of which can be considered together and might result in a date of disposal before emigration (*Furniss v Dawson* [1984] STC 153). In particular Lord Bridge's comments in this case are of interest.

> When one moves however from a single transaction to a series of inter dependent transactions designed to produce a given result it is, in my opinion, perfectly legitimate to draw a distinction between the substance and the form of the composite transaction without in any way suggesting that any of the single transactions which make up the whole are other than genuine. This has been the approach of the United States Federal Courts enabling them to develop a doctrine whereby the tax consequences of the composite transactions are dependent on its substance and not its form. I shall not attempt to review the American authorities nor do I propose a wholesale importation of the American doctrine in all its ramifications into English law. But I do suggest that the distinction between form and substance is one which can usefully be drawn in determining the tax consequences of composite transactions and one which will help to free the Courts from the shackles which have for so long been thought to be imposed on them by the Westminster case.

The *Westminster* case held that the form of a transaction takes precedence over its substance in taxation matters. (*IRC v Duke of*

Westminster [1936] 19 TC 490); this applies only in the absence of a pre-ordained series of transactions or one single composite transaction.

This warning having been given, it is obviously possible to enter into negotiations before leaving the United Kingdom which do not amount to a contract to dispose of the shares or business and to conclude these arrangements by a contract for sale after having become neither resident nor ordinarily resident in the United Kingdom. As has been explained earlier, to acquire non-ordinary residence will normally require a period of absence from the United Kingdom of at least three complete tax years. However, the Inland Revenue in a letter dated 10 July 1979, quoted in *Moores Rowland's Yellow Tax Guide*, stated:

> I can confirm that where an employee left the UK on 4 April 1979 and did not return until 6 April 1980 and was on a full-time service contract throughout that period he would be regarded as not resident and not ordinarily resident in the UK throughout the year 1979/80.

> However this practice would not be extended to a taxpayer who was only partly in employment and partly self-employed during a similar period. In such circumstances the normal rules for determining an individual's residence status would apply and on the basis that no visits were made during the intervening period the taxpayer would be regarded as not resident but ordinarily resident for the year 1979/80 in these circumstances.

'These circumstances' would be that there was not a full-time service contract covering the complete tax year.

It is obviously dangerous to rely on a full-time service contract overseas unless this can be substantiated by the facts of the case. The Revenue is unlikely to be easily persuaded that a person who has emigrated on selling his business in the United Kingdom for several million pounds is likely to take full-time employment; and a lot more is required than a mere service contract with some offshore company ostensibly requiring full-time duties, usually of a somewhat indeterminate nature.

If the emigrant disposing of the shares is not granted provisional non-resident and non-ordinarily resident status the CGT would have to be paid and recovered in due course when the non-resident and non-ordinarily resident status was established, retrospectively to include the date of disposal.

In the case of a disposal of an unincorporated business, as opposed to shares, it is important to remember that a business carried on by a non-resident through a branch or agency in the United Kingdom remains subject to UK CGT under TCGA 1992, s 10. It is therefore necessary for the business to cease while the owner is still resident in the United Kingdom and for him then to depart and thereafter conclude the disposal of the business assets, including goodwill of the former business. This is not easy to do without having entered into a binding contract before leaving the United Kingdom despite what the paperwork may purport to provide. In such circumstances it might even be more practical to transfer the business into a company in exchange for shares and claim the roll-over under the provisions of TCGA 1992, s 162, then to emigrate, and then to sell the shares in the UK company. The transfer to the company should be done before entering into any negotiations with possible purchasers, otherwise this would be regarded as a series of transactions within the *Furniss v Dawson* principle. Alternatively, it might be possible to show that the purchasers required the protection of limited liability so that this was the business purpose for the transfer of the business to a company.

Rather than try and argue that the contract was actually entered into after leaving the United Kingdom it might well be preferable to give the intended purchaser an option enabling him to acquire the shares after the vendor has become non-resident (TCGA 1992, s 28(2)). 'Conditional contract' refers in particular to a contract conditional on the exercise of an option and makes it clear that the date of the disposal is the date the option is *exercised*. It is tempting to consider entering into a put and call option, but the Revenue has argued strongly in the case of development land tax transactions that a put and call option is the equivalent of a contract for sale and that they are entitled to treat it as a disposal at the date the option was entered into.

If it is not possible to postpone the date of the contract for disposal until the vendor has become non-resident it might be possible to take a large proportion of the proceeds in the form of loan stock. If it can be shown that there is a good commercial reason for the issue of loan stock a claim for roll-over relief on the disposal of the shares should be available under TCGA 1992, s 135, with clearance under s 138. If clearance is obtained it should be possible for the vendor to become non-resident and then dispose of the loan stock, thus crystallising the gain on the shares rolled into the loan stock. It is probably unwise to arrange before departure from the United Kingdom for the loan stock immediately to be redeemed or placed with some financial institution, as the Revenue could then argue that the issue of the loan stock was merely an inserted step in what was in reality a sale for cash, again relying on *Furniss v Dawson*.

It should be noted that capital gains on Lloyd's investments as an underwriting name are basically subject to CGT as arising from a business carried on in the United Kingdom through an agent (TCGA 1992, s 10). However, syndicate investments which form part of the Lloyd's American Trust Fund and Lloyd's Canadian Trust Fund are regarded as not situated in the United Kingdom and non-UK securities in the Lloyd's sterling trust fund are also regarded as situated outside the United Kingdom. Exempt gilts held as part of a Lloyd's fund would retain their CGT exemption.

6.6 Foreign taxes

It is beyond the scope of this book to consider non-UK tax liabilities, but if a business or shares are sold after having left the United Kingdom the taxpayer may well have become resident in some other country which imposes a CGT charge or assesses capital gains as income. The general advice given with regard to UK CGT may be overruled if the effective rate of overseas tax on the chargeable gain would be greater.

Local advice should be taken before concluding the contract for disposal, as to whether there is a potential tax charge in the country of residence, and if so what, if anything, can be done about it.

6.7 Trusts

The UK resident beneficiary of a non-resident trust is liable to CGT if the settlor was UK domiciled and resident when he made the settlement and if the beneficiary is resident when the gain is distributed to him. If, however, the beneficiary is not domiciled in the United Kingdom, TCGA 1992, s 87(7) exempts him from a CGT charge. See also Chapter 8.

6.8 Offshore funds

Before 1984, it was possible for a UK resident to invest in certain offshore funds known as 'roll-up funds', where income to the funds was not distributed but accumulated tax free — when the investment was realised the accumulated profit, both gain and income, was subject to UK CGT only. Complicated rules were introduced to take effect from 1 January 1984 (FA 1984, ss 92–100, now incorporated into TA 1988, ss 757–764) which means that a UK resident investor is now liable to tax on his entire gain in an offshore 'roll-up' fund as if it were income, under Schedule D, Case VI. If the investor is domiciled outside the United Kingdom the tax liability will only apply to any gain actually remitted to the United Kingdom.

In the case of a UK expatriate there will be no liability to UK tax on realisations of gain from a 'roll-up' fund, so long as he remains non-resident and non-ordinarily resident in the United Kingdom, but realisations of gain after he returns home will attract the full liability to UK income tax. This future heavy exposure to UK taxation can be avoided by investing in offshore funds that have been granted 'distributor status'. The Finance Act 1984 provided that where a fund meets certain rules — the most important is that the fund must distribute at least 85 per cent of the income received — the investor will be taxed on his income and gain in the normal way, ie Schedule D, Case VI in respect of the income distribution and CGT in respect of realised growth.

6.9 Gifts from non-residents

If an asset given by a non-resident to a UK resident is subsequently disposed of by the donee, the donee is treated as acquiring the asset at market value at the time of the gift, and is liable to CGT only on any excess over the acquisition value.

6.10 Non-sterling bank accounts

Under TCGA 1992, s 275(1) a non-sterling bank account belonging to a non-UK domiciled individual is treated as located outside the United Kingdom and therefore exempt from CGT on currency movements unless the account is held at the UK branch of a bank and the individual is resident in the United Kingdom.

6.11 UK investment managers

An investment manager in the United Kingdom whose normal business it is to buy, sell and manage investments on behalf of a non-resident with whom he is not connected is normally protected from a UK tax charge by the provisions of TMA 1970, s 78. There are cases where the protection can be lost, such as if the transactions can be taxed as part of a wider trade (insurance, for example) carried on in the United Kingdom through the same agency. The Revenue has spelt out the rules in detail in a statement of practice (SP 15/91), which examines the connected persons rules and trading and investment transactions in the context of the agency relief.

7 Inheritance tax

As has already been seen, the non-resident working expatriate can, to a very great extent, avoid any liability to UK income tax and CGT. The main determinant of liability for income tax, apart from the location of the income source, is the individual's residence for tax purposes, and CGT is generally only chargeable on persons resident or ordinarily resident in the United Kingdom. This is not the case for IHT.

A charge to IHT may arise whenever there is a transfer of assets, (other than lifetime gifts to an individual (or certain kinds of trust) made more than seven years before the donor's death), no matter where the assets are located, made by a person who is, or was at death, domiciled or deemed to be domiciled (see Chapter 1) in the United Kingdom. In addition, IHT may be charged on a transfer of assets located in the United Kingdom by a person not domiciled in the United Kingdom.

So far as most British expatriates are concerned, although they may be non-resident for many years, their domicile remains the United Kingdom and, in consequence, they remain liable to IHT.

What follows is a necessarily brief outline of IHT with the emphasis placed on those aspects which are likely to be of greatest interest or relevance to expatriates. More detailed information is to be found in this book's companion volumes, the *Allied Dunbar Tax Guide* and the *Allied Dunbar Capital Taxes and Estate Planning Guide*.

Note:
It is important to remember that expatriates who do manage to change their legal domicile from the United Kingdom remain liable for IHT for three years following that change because of the 'deemed domicile' provisions described in Chapter 1.

7.1   Chargeable transfers

Inheritance tax may be payable whenever there is a chargeable transfer of assets. In general terms, a chargeable transfer is one which reduces the value of the transferor's total assets or his estate: in general parlance, a gift or bequest. Tax is chargeable on the cumulative total of chargeable transfers made during the donor's lifetime and on the value of his estate at death. The period of accumulation is restricted to seven years, ie in year 8, the cumulative total of transfers made will be those of years 2 to 8, and transfers made in year 1 will drop out of account. Following death, the IHT due will be calculated on the value of the estate at death plus chargeable transfers made in the preceding seven years.

For transfers on or after 10 March 1992 the first £150,000 is charged at a nil rate and the excess is charged on death at 40 per cent and on lifetime transfers at a reducing percentage of the 40 per cent rate, depending upon the number of years between the transfer and the death of the donor. Up to three years the full rate is payable, four years is reduced to 80 per cent, five years 60 per cent, six years 40 per cent, seven years 20 per cent and thereafter no IHT is due.

Following death, chargeable transfers made within the previous seven years are reassessed and the additional tax then becomes payable, but there is no revaluation of the asset transferred at the date of death.

It is fundamental to an understanding of IHT to appreciate that the amount of tax payable is calculated by reference to the total loss to the donor, ie, the amount by which his estate has been reduced by the transfer. It is not the value of the gift in isolation. In practice, this is of greatest importance in connection with unquoted shares. If a father has 55 per cent of the shares in a family company and transfers 10 per cent to discretionary trust, those shares might be worth, say, £100 per share as a small minority interest. However, the father's shareholding has fallen from a 55 per cent controlling interest (shares worth £500 each) to a 45 per cent large minority holding (shares worth, say, £300 each). If there were 10,000 shares in issue, the chargeable transfer (loss to the father's estate) would be not £10,000 (1,000 × £100) but £1,400,000 (from 5,500 × £500 to 4,500 × £300).

7.2   Exemptions and reliefs

The IHT legislation contains many provisions exempting certain transfers of value from tax. The most important of these are described below.

7.3   Potentially exempt transfers

A lifetime transfer by an individual to another individual is a potentially exempt transfer (PET). This means that if the transferor survives for seven years it is exempt, but if he dies within seven years it is chargeable. This also applies to transfers to an interest in possession trust, an accumulation and maintenance trust or a trust for a disabled person.

7.4   Transfers between spouses

Where both spouses are domiciled in the United Kingdom any transfer of assets between them is exempt. Where the recipient spouse is not domiciled in the United Kingdom at the time of the transfer, the total exemption is restricted to £55,000 (by IHTA 1984, s 18(2)) — (see also later). Additional transfers would fall first into the usual zero rate band. The practical effect of this is that for transfers on or after 10 March 1992, no tax is charged on the first £205,000 of the estate. The spouse exemption applies to both lifetime transfers and transfers at death. There is no similar restriction in other cases where the transferee is non-UK domiciled and the transferor is domiciled in the United Kingdom. This may give rise to opportunities for channelling gifts through a non-UK domiciled individual who subsequently settles a discretionary trust, subject to anti-avoidance provisions in IHTA 1984, s 268 and the extended definition of settlor in IHTA 1984, s 44.

7.5   Annual allowances

A person may make as many small gifts to as many people as he wishes in a year without incurring any IHT. In order to qualify for this exemption, the maximum gift to any individual in the year is £250 (IHTA 1984, s 20(1)). If the gift is greater than £250 it will be taxable unless it can be covered by one of the other exemptions described below. In addition to the small gifts allowance, there is an annual allowance of £3,000 (IHTA 1984, s 19). This allowance, to the extent that it is unused in the year, may be carried forward for one year only. However, where an annual allowance or part of that allowance is carried forward it can only be used once the annual allowance for the second year has, itself, been exhausted.

Example: Inheritance tax — annual allowance

A does not expect to live long and gives £2,000 to her daughter in Year 1; she makes no other transfers in that year and therefore has an annual allowance totalling £4,000 in Year 2. If, however, she only gives away £2,000 in that year, her surplus to carry forward to Year 3 is not £2,000, but £1,000 again. She has lost the amount carried forward from Year 1 because she did not fully utilise her Year 2 allowance. Had she given £3,000 in Year 2 she would have nothing to carry foward.

These annual allowances are available separately to husband and wife and the value of the gift is calculated without tax, ie it is not grossed up. These allowances are available only against lifetime transfers.

7.6　Normal expenditure out of income

A gift made during a person's lifetime will be exempt if it is shown:

(1)　to be part of that person's habitual expenditure;
(2)　that, taking one year with another, it is made out of income; and
(3)　that allowing for all such transfers out of income, the transferor is left with sufficient income to maintain his usual standard of living.

On the occasion of the first gift of income it will be considered as exempt if there is clear evidence of further gifts to be made, such as insurance policy premiums on a policy written in trust (IHTA 1984, s 21).

7.7　Gifts in consideration of marriage

Wedding gifts into trust or within seven years of death are exempt so far as they fall within the following limits:

(1)　up to £5,000 from a parent of either party to the marriage;
(2)　up to £2,500 from one party to the marriage to the other or from grandparents or remoter ancestors of either party;

(3)   up to £1,000 in any other case.

As with the two previous exemptions, this one is also only available for gifts made during the donor's lifetime (IHTA 1984, s 22).

7.8   Dispositions for maintenance of family

This exemption applies to dispositions from one spouse to another and includes any made on the dissolution of a marriage (IHTA 1984, s 11). It also covers those made for the children of either spouse (including any illegitimate child of the transferor) until the end of the tax year in which the child attains the age of 18 or, if later, until the child finishes full-time education or training. Where any person makes a disposition to a child who has been in that person's care for a substantial period, the exemption also applies, even though the person is not the child's parent. Finally, the exemption applies for the maintenance of a dependent relative and, by concession, to a disposition from a child to his or her unmarried mother who is financially dependent on the child.

7.9   Other exempt transfers

The previous exemptions have primarily concerned transfers to individuals which are in any case exempt if made more than seven years before death. There are several other exempt transfers of a more impersonal nature. These include transfers to charities, gifts for national purposes, to political parties and for the public benefit (IHTA 1984, ss 23–26).

Finally no IHT is payable on the estate of anyone who dies from a wound, accident, or disease contracted while on active service (IHTA 1984, s 154). By concession, this exemption is extended to the estates of members of the Royal Ulster Constabulary where death is as a result of terrorist activities in Northern Ireland.

7.10   Business property relief

Relief is given for the transfer of certain property which is 'relevant business property' by way of a reduction in the valuation of the property under IHTA 1984, ss 103–114. Before relief can be given, there are certain conditions to be met. As well as being relevant business property, the transfer must be of property from a qualifying business (basically a business carried on for gain other than a business which is primarily concerned with dealing in land or securities or holding investments), and the property must have been owned for a period of at least two years prior to the transfer.

Relevant business property falls into four classes:

(1)　unincorporated business — property comprising a business or interest in a business attracts relief of 100 per cent;

(2)　shares or securities — if these gave the transferor control of a company or if the company was an unquoted company and they gave more than 25 per cent of the voting rights, they also attract relief at 100 per cent immediately before the transfer;

(3)　land, buildings, machinery or plant used in a partnership or a controlled company or, by the transferor, which was settled property in which he was entitled to an interest in possession — relief is at 50 per cent;

(4)　unquoted minority shareholdings — these attract relief at 50 per cent.

Note:
In (2) and (4) above a company is still considered to be 'quoted' if its shares are dealt in on the Unlisted Securities Market (USM).

7.11　Agricultural property relief

Agricultural property in the United Kingdom, the Channel Islands or the Isle of Man attracts relief at 100 per cent under IHTA 1984, ss 115–124 where it has been occupied for the two years before the transfer by the transferor for the purposes of agriculture, or where it was owned for the seven years before the transfer but farmed by persons other than the transferor. A further condition to be satisfied for the 100 per cent relief is that the transferor must enjoy vacant possession or be entitled to it within 12 months. In other cases the relief is restricted to 50 per cent.

7.12　Potentially exempt lifetime transfers of agricultural and business property

In circumstances where such transfers become taxable due to the death within seven years of the transferor, the conditions necessary for obtaining the relief must still be met at the date of death. Effectively, therefore, the recipient of such transfers must continue to own the property and continue to use it in the manner which qualifies it for relief for seven years after the transfer, or risk forfeiting the relief.

7.13 Persons not domiciled in the United Kingdom

Overseas assets owned by persons not domiciled in the United Kingdom are generally excluded property for the purposes of IHT (IHTA 1984, s 6(1)). That is, any transfer of such property will not give rise to a liability. However, where such persons own assets in the United Kingdom, then any transfer of such assets may give rise to a charge to tax. There are, as usual, several exemptions and reliefs available to offset this general rule, in addition to the general potential exemption for transfers to indivdiuals.

Under a double taxation agreement, property may be deemed to be located abroad, thus making it excluded property (see Chapter 11). The property of members of visiting forces or of staff of allied headquarters is excluded property. Where a person holds certain UK government securities, then these will be excluded property if the holder is not domiciled and not ordinarily resident in the United Kingdom (IHTA 1984, s 6(2)). For this latter exclusion, it is legal domicile as opposed to the artificial deemed domicile which applies (IHTA 1984, s 267(2)).

Where overseas property is settled property, it will only be excluded property if at the time the settlement was made the settlor was not domiciled in the United Kingdom (IHTA 1984, s 48(3)(*b*)). If that is not the case then the settled property will not be excluded, regardless of any subsequent change of domicile of the settlor and regardless of the domicile of any beneficiaries. A reversionary interest in overseas settled property does not come under these rules but is determined according to the general rule which is that if the person beneficially entitled to the reversionary interest is domiciled in the United Kingdom, there is a liability, and if he is not, then it is excluded property (IHTA 1984, s 48(1)).

7.14 Location of assets

Where an asset is located has to be determined according to the laws of England and Wales, Scotland or Northern Ireland except where these are superseded by special provisions in a double taxation agreement. The commoner types of assets are normally considered to be situated as follows:

(1) cash — where physically located;
(2) bank accounts — the location of the bank or branch (note: foreign currency accounts owned by a non-UK domiciled person but held in the United Kingdom are exempt);
(3) registered securities — the location of the share register;
(4) bearer securities — the location of the title documents;
(5) land and buildings — their actual location;
(6) business assets — the place where the business is conducted;
(7) debts — the residence of the debtor (or for specialty debts, such as a life assurance policy issued under seal, the place where the document evidencing the debt is located and, for judgment debts, the country where the judgment is recorded).

7.15   The non-UK domiciled spouse

Before 1 January 1974, a wife assumed her husband's domicile on marriage. When the marriage ended, either by death or divorce, the wife retained her husband's domicile unless and until she acquired a new domicile of choice. The current position of women married before 1 January 1974 is that they retain their husbands' domicile (originally a domicile of dependence) as their deemed domicile of choice until, by their own positive actions, they acquire a new domicile of choice. For marriages contracted after 1 January 1974, a wife has had complete independence of domicile and will retain her domicile of origin or any pre-marriage domicile of dependence until she chooses to acquire a new domicile of choice which may or may not be the same as her husband's domicile.

For IHT purposes, a couple of mixed domicile (where one of them is domiciled in the United Kingdom and the other is not) have to take extra care in their tax planning. Their situation does, however, offer some opportunities not available to couples where both are UK domiciled.

Dealing first of all with the restrictions, it has already been mentioned that a transfer from a spouse domiciled in the United Kingdom to one who is not so domiciled, is exempt only up to a total transfer of £55,000. The reason behind this is obviously to prevent the avoidance of tax which would arise by simply using the non-domiciled spouse as a conduit for transfers of non-UK sited assets to other parties such as children. Nonetheless, substantial value can still be transferred because the UK domiciled spouse will have, in addition to the £55,000 exemption, an additional amount of £150,000 which on transfer will be within the nil rate band. Further transfers may be made using the annual allowance and any subsequent increases in the exempt allowance or the width of the nil rate band. After seven years, the £150,000 transferred initially within the nil rate band will fall out of account.

Where the spouse who is not domiciled in the United Kingdom makes any gifts or transfers, there will be no IHT liability so long as the property concerned is excluded property — generally property located outside the United Kingdom. One possible pitfall for the non-UK domiciled spouse arises following the family's assumption or resumption of residence in the United Kingdom. The Inland Revenue may seek to claim that the originally non-domiciled spouse has acquired a new domicile of choice in the United Kingdom. However, they cannot have it both ways. There is a great reluctance in the absence of very strong evidence to accept that a person has shed his or her UK domicile — it should follow, therefore, that there should be equal reluctance to accept that a person has shed a non-UK domicile of origin and acquired UK domicile by choice. But as with most aspects of British taxation, the onus is on the individual to prove the Revenue wrong. The pointers to a change of domicile given earlier should be considered in this light.

In any event, even the person accepted as not being domiciled in the United Kingdom in the legal sense, will be deemed to be so domiciled for IHT purposes after a period of 17 years residence here. Strictly, the requirement is to have been resident in the United Kingdom in not less than 17 out of the 20 years of assessment ending with that in which the chargeable transfer occurs.

7.16 Settled property

If the IHT rules are generally seen as very complex, this is nowhere more true than when considering the question of settled property. There are several types of trusts or settlements which have a useful application for IHT mitigation and these are discussed in some detail below, in Chapter 8.

For details of the settled property provisions, reference must be made to more specialist textbooks but the following points illuminate, however briefly, some important aspects.

Generally, settlements are themselves subject to IHT at lifetime rates if, when the settlement was made, the settlor was domiciled in the United Kingdom. The settlement of any property after 26 March 1974 is a chargeable transfer by the settlor (assuming he is domiciled in the United Kingdom) unless the trust is for transfers into an interest in possession trust, an accumulation or maintenance trust or a trust for a disabled person: these are potentially exempt transfers. A person having an interest in possession in any property, is deemed to possess that property for IHT purposes so that when that interest ends, there is deemed to be a potentially exempt transfer of the value of the property, under IHTA 1984, ss 49–53. There is no chargeable or potentially exempt transfer if a person becomes absolutely entitled to the property in which he previously had an interest in possession. The special rules relating to discretionary trusts and accumulation and maintenance trusts are discussed later.

A reversionary interest in a settlement of UK property is excluded property under IHTA 1984, s 48(1) unless it had been acquired for value, is one in which the settlor or his spouse has a beneficial interest or is a reversionary interest under a lease for life treated as a settlement.

7.17 Inheritance tax planning

For every tax, there soon springs up a tax avoidance scheme, or many of them. This continuing game between legislators and tax consultants is as obvious in the area of IHT as anywhere else although the Revenue's success in ignoring purely fiscal moves in a composite transaction in *Furniss v Dawson* [1984] STC 153 should be noted.

As stated at the beginning of this chapter, the recast IHT is in some aspects similar to estate duty (the predecessor to CTT), which was considerably easier to avoid than the tax which replaced it. On the other hand, the ease of avoiding IHT — by simply making gifts to individuals more than seven years before death — depends on the donor's ability to make outright gifts and lose the benefit of the associated income, because it is no longer possible, as with CTT, to make gifts with reservation of interest.

Basic IHT planning is very straightforward, such as simply making use of the various exemptions and reliefs particularly the exemption for lifetime gifts to individuals. However, rather than merely disposing of cash, some thought might be given to transferring assets which might be expected to grow in value but which have a relatively low value at the time of transfer. Another frequent suggestion is the equalisation of estate between husband and wife with the first to die leaving a substantial part of his or her estate other than to the spouse. In this way maximum use can be made of each spouse's entitlement to allowances and the nil rate band.

Example: Inheritance tax — estate planning

A husband has an estate worth £260,000 and the wife £40,000; in their wills each leaves his or her estate to the other. On the second death, everything goes to the children. Under these provisions there would be no IHT payable on the first death and, assuming no previous chargeable transfers, an IHT charge of £60,000 on the second death. If, however the husband transferred £110,000 to his wife during his lifetime and they each decided to leave £150,000 to their children with the balance to the spouse, there would still be no IHT to pay on the first death and on the second death, when the estate is £150,000, the IHT payable would be nil, a saving of £60,000.

One reason for equalising the estates rather than simply making enough available for the wife to use the nil rate band is to allow maximum flexibility on the first death following which a written variation of the will (see later) could be used in the light of prevailing circumstances.

The transferor should not so reduce his estate that the surviving spouse cannot sustain a required standard of living. In addition, payment of IHT should be postponed from the date of the first death to the second death by leaving the estate on the excess over the nil rate band to the surviving spouse.

7.18   Insurance policies

To use these policies, the transferor or the intending transferor effects a policy on his life written in trust for his beneficiaries. The sum assured under such a policy should be the amount of the anticipated IHT which will be due on the estate passing at death. Where there is a relatively short period of liability to the tax as, for example, when a person emigrates permanently but remains deemed domiciled in the United Kingdom for three years, a three year term policy would be the cheapest and simplest form of IHT protection. Similarly, if a major transfer of assets is made to take advantage of the lower lifetime rates of tax, it may be worth insuring for the difference between the tax paid, if any, and the tax which would become payable if death occurred within seven years of that transfer. In most circumstances however, a term policy is unlikely to be the wisest course because as the potential transferor gets older renewing the policy can become very expensive. A better solution is to take out a whole of life policy and write it in trust at a reasonably early stage. Premiums paid by the life assured/settlor in respect of the policy in trust are, of course, transfers of value into the trust and hence can amount to either immediately chargeable transfers or potentially exempt transfers depending on whether the trust is a discretionary trust. However, the exemption for gifts out of income and where necessary, the £3,000 annual exemption can normally be applied to those transfers of premium and, where this is so, the payments will be totally exempt. These exemptions can also be applied to the premiums paid on an investment oriented policy written in trust and this, too, can be a useful way of transferring a growing asset to others.

7.19　The family home

One asset which can sometimes prove difficult to plan for effectively is the family home, and for many people this is their main asset. Normally a couple will own their house as joint tenants. On the death of one of them the deceased's share is automatically transferred to the survivor. Assuming the couple are married, and are both either UK or non-UK domiciled, there will be no IHT payable on this occasion but on the second death, the whole value of the house will be counted in calculating the tax. The effect of this is illustrated in the following example.

Example: Inheritance tax — the family home

A couple have joint net assets of £390,000, of which £300,000 represents the value of their house, the remaining £90,000 being invested to provide income. The house is owned under a joint tenancy and each holds about £45,000 of investments. Under their wills each leaves his or her estate to the other. The couple have two children who will inherit everything on the second death. Because the survivor after the first death will still require a similar income, it is not practicable to leave anything to the children on that occasion so the eventual IHT bill will be £96,000.

The bill can, however, be reduced by changing the way the house is owned. If the couple own the house as tenants in common, rather than as joint tenants, their individual shares do not automatically go to the other on death but may be dealt with in the same way as any other asset. Thus, in the previous example, although the income producing assets could not be left to the children, a share of the house could be.

If, on the death of the first spouse his or her half-share in the house was left to the children, this would be a chargeable transfer of £150,000 with no IHT payable. The estate on the second death would be £240,000 on which the IHT would be £36,000, a saving of £60,000.

But tenancies in common are not without their drawbacks. There must be a high degree of trust among all the parties so that the widow or widower can continue to live in the property only half of which she or he will own. There can also be a problem if the co-owner is declared bankrupt. It is very important for anyone contemplating such an arrangement to discuss it fully with his solicitor who will also give an indication of the cost of changing an existing joint tenancy to a tenancy in common, which usually requires only a simple notice of severance served on the co-owner.

8 Wills, settlements and trusts

8.1 Wills and assets in more than one jurisdiction

Anyone whose assets are other than negligible should make a properly drawn up and witnessed will, unless he has no concern about the disposition of those assets after his death. Anyone who dies without leaving a valid will dies intestate, and his property will be disposed of according to the laws of intestacy. This procedure will seldom coincide with the deceased's wishes. This is especially true if the deceased held assets in more than one jurisdiction. Not only that, but intestacy may also give rise to prolonged legal arguments and transactions, which in some countries have been known to go on for half a century or more.

This brings out an important point for the expatriate, particularly. If he has UK domicile, he should not only have a valid UK will which allocates all his worldwide property according to his wishes, but he should also have a will covering any assets held outside the United Kingdom which is valid in the jurisdiction where those assets are held.

Under private international law, where there is a will, the passing of assets from the deceased's estate to his heirs is governed by the law of the deceased's domicile in the case of movable property (such as bank deposits or securities) and by the local law in the case of immovable property. It will often be the case, therefore, that any decision of, say, an English court relating to immovable property overseas will not be effective in the overseas jurisdiction until it has been approved by a court there. The overseas court may also insist on a local grant of probate or Letters of Administration, which can be a relatively expensive procedure.

A further point to bear in mind about assets held overseas is that not all countries allow the testator complete freedom to dispose as he pleases. In many countries the children of the deceased are legally entitled to inherit a minimum portion of the estate, or of part of the estate. In other countries, the incidence of estate duties or IHT varies according to the kinship or other relationship of the heirs to the deceased. Even in the United Kingdom, with very liberal laws in this respect, a will may be challenged and the dispositions altered by the court if, for instance, no provision has been made for a person who was financially dependent on the deceased. A will may be challenged in the United Kingdom on several other grounds also, but this matter lies beyond the scope of the present Guide.

It will be clear even from the above simple generalisations that the administration of an overseas estate can be an extremely complex business. But one thing is certain: the trouble and expense (in the way of legal fees payable both in the United Kingdom and elsewhere) incurred in sorting matters out properly in advance amount to a mere fraction of the trouble and expense that will be incurred by the executors or administrators if proper arrangements have not been made. Indeed, an individual with assets in more than one country owes it morally to his executors as well as his heirs to make proper arrangements, even if this means writing several wills and consulting with several lawyers in several jurisdictions.

Apart from the simple efficiency in dealing with a local estate under local law that only a locally acceptable document makes possible, there are two further important practical points. First, proper testamentary arrangements regularly reviewed are essential to IHT or estate duty planning. They are the only way to protect the heirs from the full ravages of taxation. Secondly, from the UK viewpoint, a grant of probate or Letters of Administration will not be given until any IHT has been paid. Since assets will not normally be released until the grant is made, the only way to pay the tax bill is to borrow the money. If overseas assets can be speedily released through a local probate, these can be used to pay the UK tax and thereby hasten the release of assets held in the United Kingdom.

8.2 Will trusts

A UK will may grant an absolute interest to a beneficiary or may create a will trust under which the assets are left to trustees for the benefit of various beneficiaries. The types of possible trust are discussed below. The most common will trust is to leave the majority of the estate to the surviving spouse for her life with remainder to the children or grandchildren. The advantage of this arrangement is that the life interest to the surviving spouse is treated for IHT purposes as her absolute interest and therefore the IHT exemption on leaving assets to a surviving spouse still applies. However, the ultimate destination of the assets is assured so that should, for example, the wife re-marry and have further children by the second marriage, the deceased former husband's estate passes through to his own children and cannot be diverted to the children of the second marriage. It is possible to leave the reversionary interest to the grandchildren rather than to the children and so avoid an IHT charge on the death of the children. Whether this is desirable of course depends on the children's assets and the respective ages of the parties.

8.3 Incidence of inheritance tax

It is also important to bear in mind when drafting the will the incidence of IHT. Section 211 of IHTA 1984 following *Re Dougal* [1981] STC 514 makes it clear that IHT on death in respect of personal property and of real property in the United Kingdom is a general testamentary expense payable out of residue in the absence of contrary provisions in the will. If, therefore, the intention is that any legacy should bear its own share of IHT, it is important that the will makes this clear. There are complicated provisions in IHTA 1984, ss 38–42 to deal with the case where part of the residue is left on an exempt legacy such as to the surviving spouse, and part on a chargeable legacy such as to the children.

Overseas assets subject to IHT will normally be subject to their proportionate share of the IHT applicable thereto. For the avoidance of doubt, it is preferable to draft the will so that it is made perfectly clear which, if any, legacies are to bear their share of IHT.

As already noted, the provisions of a will can largely determine the amount of IHT which will fall due. A will can, in fact, be looked upon as an IHT planning tool. However, if family circumstances at the date of death are significantly different from what was envisaged when the will was prepared, or if the will is highly inefficient in a tax-planning sense, the will provisions may be altered by a written variation. If this is done within two years of death, no IHT will be charged on the variations or rearrangements if the parties concerned so elect, and the tax payable will be computed on the basis that the varied provisions were effective at death. Stamp duty is no longer payable on the value transferred under a written variation (FA 1985, s 85).

8.4 Written variations

The problem with the written variation is that it requires any beneficiary whose share is being reduced to be legally competent (ie adult and of sound mind), as any attempts so to modify the interest of a child beneficiary would require the consent of the Court. In practice, it may be preferable to leave that part of the estate which, for example, may or may not be required by the surviving spouse to trustees of a discretionary settlement with the intention that the trustees would, within two years of the date of death, redistribute the assets among the various beneficiaries in accordance with their needs.

Written variations are treated for IHT purposes as a disposition on death under IHTA 1984, ss 17 and 142 and for CGT purposes by TCGA 1992, s 62(6). However, for income tax purposes, the income in the period from the date of death to the date of the variation (or distribution from any discretionary trust) remains that of the original beneficiaries. It is also likely that a variation in favour of children would be argued by the Revenue to be an indirect settlement by the original beneficiary so that, for income tax purposes, any income distributed to the child during his minority would be treated as the income of the parent under TA 1988, s 663. A variation or two-year discretionary trust should therefore be regarded as a useful opportunity to fine tune the dispositions given by will rather than a substitute for a carefully planned will reviewed at frequent intervals.

Example: Inheritance tax — written variation

Mr Bird died in July 1992. His net estate was valued at £400,000 including a house worth £100,000. Apart from £25,000 to his son, the estate was left to Mr Bird's widow. When Mr Bird's will was drawn up many years previously the value of his estate was only about £150,000 with the house worth £50,000. He felt at the time that his widow would require £75,000 to provide her income and that was his rationale for the structuring of his will.

As it happens, in 1992, there will be no IHT to pay following Mr Bird's death (he has made no previous transfers) but there is a potential tax charge on Mrs Bird's death, assuming she leaves her estate to the son (she has personal assets worth

£50,000) of £110,000. She and her son therefore effect a written variation whereby the son receives £140,000 instead of £25,000 and his children receive £10,000 in total. There is still no IHT payable on the estate. The potential charge on the death of Mrs Bird is reduced from £110,000 (on £425,000) to £60,000 (on £300,000). The written variation has therefore saved IHT of £50,000.

8.5   Trusts

A trust or settlement is a legal relationship which is established when a person transfers assets into the care of others for the benefit of a third party. The three parties concerned in this relationship, the settlor, trustees, and beneficiaries respectively, may all incur tax liabilities stemming from the trust in different ways. A detailed explanation of trust law is beyond the scope of this book and readers are referred to the *Allied Dunbar Capital Taxes and Estate Planning Guide* for further information. Trusts constitute an extremely complex area of the law and good professional advice is essential.

This chapter can only provide an outline of the major tax planning aspects of trusts as they affect, or might affect, the expatriate. It must be stressed that to establish a trust is not a job for a layman. Perhaps more than in any other field of tax planning, trust work requires the assistance of expert professional advice.

8.5.1   The residence of trusts

For most income tax purposes, a trust with a UK resident, ordinarily resident or domiciled settlor at the time of creation is resident outside the United Kingdom only if all the trustees are themselves so resident and the administration and management of the trust are carried out overseas, TA 1989, s 110 (*Kelly v Rogers* (1935) 19 TC 692, *Reid's Trustees v IRC* (1929) 14 TC 512). If there is a UK resident trustee of a trust settled by a non-UK resident and domiciled settlor which also has a foreign trustee, the UK resident trustee is deemed to be non-resident for income tax purposes (FA 1989, s 110(1)(*b*)). Similar provisions apply to personal representatives under FA 1989, s 111. For CGT purposes, TCGA 1992, s 69(1) only requires a majority of trustees to be non-UK resident. A trust which is not resident in the United Kingdom may enjoy substantial tax advantages over the domestic settlement but there are numerous provisions in the UK legislation which seek to prevent tax avoidance by the use of such vehicles by or for the benefit of persons ordinarily resident in the United Kingdom. The three main UK taxes income tax, CGT and IHT can each have an impact on trusts and on each of the parties involved. Tax liabilities are determined not only by the residence of the trust and the individuals concerned but also by the type of trust which is involved. The following section on the taxation of trusts outlines the tax consequences which attach to each of the main types of trust with which the expatriate may be concerned.

8.5.2 Resident trusts

It may be useful to make the first distinction between types of trusts as between those where the settlor is alive and those where he is deceased. The main thrust of the anti-avoidance legislation is concerned with preventing a settlor using a trust mechanism to provide himself with a tax-sheltered 'piggy bank' for his own or his wife's benefit. To that end there are numerous provisions which seek to tax trust income as that of the settlor and these are described below. Where the settlor has died, whether the trust was set up during his lifetime or under his will, the taxation rules are somewhat less complex.

In general terms, a UK trust is liable for basic rate income tax on all its income, wherever arising. Where trust income has already suffered tax at source or is accompanied by a tax credit, this will be accounted for in the trust assessment. Where the trust has overseas income which has been taxed abroad then relief for double taxation may be available either to the trustees or the beneficiaries. The income of discretionary trusts and accumulation trusts, after deducting expenses, is also liable for an additional charge (10 per cent) — TA 1988, s 686. The income tax assessment of trusts is generally made in the name of the trustees and the tax due is payable out of the trust funds. Where trust income is distributed to beneficiaries it is treated as received net of tax at 35 per cent under TA 1988, s 687 (or 25 per cent in the case of a beneficiary absolutely entitled to the income, that is where the trust is not a discretionary trust).

A non-resident trust is liable to UK tax on its UK income at the basic rate and, on accumulations, at the additional rate as well. See *IRC v Regent Trust Co Ltd* [1980] STC 140.

Trusts are also liable for CGT in much the same way as individuals but the annual exemption is restricted to 50 per cent of that available to individuals. For 1992/93, the trust exemption is therefore £2,900. For trusts formed after 6 June 1978, this exemption is split among all trusts with the same settlor, ie, if he made four trusts, each would be entitled to exemption on the first £725. For trusts formed before that date, the full £2,900 is allowed. Certain trusts for the mentally disabled and those in receipt of attendance allowances are entitled to the same exemption as an individual; TCGA 1992, Sched 1.

Some of the aspects of IHT and trusts were mentioned in the preceding chapter. *What is perhaps of the greatest importance is to note that, for IHT purposes, the residence of the trust is largely immaterial.* A trust may incur a liability to IHT on its worldwide assets if, at the time it was set up, the settlor was domiciled in the United Kingdom (IHTA 1984, s 48(3)(*a*)). If the settlor was domiciled elsewhere, the IHT liability will be restricted to transfers of trust assets located in the United Kingdom.

8.5.3 Trusts created *inter vivos*

Where a settlement is made during the lifetime of the settlor, the taxation rules are particularly rigorous to prevent the avoidance of tax. An outline of these anti-avoidance provisions is given below.

8.5.4 Income tax

The basic rule a settlor must obey in order to avoid having the trust income assessed on him, is fully to divest himself of the assets he is transferring into the trust. If he retains an interest in either the income or the assets of the trust then any income not distributed to beneficiaries will be treated as the settlor's income (TA 1988, ss 673–674). A retained interest is widely defined but generally means that the settlor or his or her spouse is able to obtain some benefit from the income or assets of the trust at any time. Even where the income is distributed to others any excess of higher rate tax over the basic rate on the distribution will be charged to the settlor.

Akin to retaining an interest is a power to revoke the trust. If the trust can be revoked in whole or in part, and on revocation the trust property reverts to the settlor or his spouse, then the income of the trust (or a part thereof corresponding to the partial revocation) will be treated as the income of the settlor (TA 1988, ss 671, 672). The power of revocation may be immediate or postponed, but in the latter case, if the power cannot be used for at least six years, the income will not be treated as that of the settlor until the power becomes exercisable. Power to revoke includes a power to advance the whole of the capital, or to diminish the assets of the trust or the income receivable by beneficiaries other than the settlor or his spouse. Whether it is the settlor or another person who has the power to revoke is immaterial.

Where there is a settlement of income such as a covenant, it is essential that the payments should be capable of being made for a period of at least six years (TA 1988, s 660). The six-year rule applies to settlements generally but is normally of particular relevance to income settlements. Where a covenant fails on this rule, it will be treated as income of the settlor and not the payee. Nevertheless, the payment will still be deemed to have been made to the covenantee and then returned to the settlor: the settlor is then treated as receiving investment income, even if the payment was made out of earned income or capital. As a result, the settlor may find that he has more tax to pay because of a failed covenant than he would had he not instituted it in the first place (*Ang v Parish* [1980] STC 341). However, since 15 March 1988 there have been no tax advantages in covenanting money to an individual.

Where a capital sum (which includes a loan or loan repayment) is paid by trustees to the settlor, his spouse, or a third party directly or indirectly at the settlor's direction, that sum is treated as the income of the settlor and is assessed on him under TA 1988, s 677. The assessment, however, is restricted to the amount of undistributed income in the trust but includes income previously accumulated. The tax charge is based on the amount of undistributed income grossed up at the basic rate plus the additional rate and credit is given for tax already charged on the trust. Where the undistributed income is less than the capital sum, there is provision to carry forward the excess of the capital sum to subsequent years. The settlor will then be charged to the extent of undistributed income in those years until the capital sum is fully extinguished. For capital payments made after 5 April 1981, the period for carry forward is restricted to eleven years (capital payments made before that date are to be treated as made on that date so as to fall within the new rules, so far as they have not been charged).

Under a discretionary trust, that is, one where the trustees may apply the trust property and/or income at their discretion, the settlor and his spouse must be specifically excluded from benefit, otherwise the income will be charged on the settlor whether or not he receives it. This does not apply where the benefit may accrue to the widow or widower of the settlor.

Settlements for the benefit of the settlor's infant children do not generally provide an income tax advantage, in view of the effects of TA 1988, s 663. The exception to this rule is an accumulation settlement: TA 1988, s 664. Any income belonging to a child which is derived from a parental source is deemed to be the income of the parent for tax purposes. This applies not only to settlements made by parents but to any transfer of assets from the parent to his or her child. For example, if a parent gave his child shares in a company any dividends paid to the child until he reached the age of majority would be treated as the parent's income. Similarly taxed too would be the interest in a child's bank account where the capital came from a parent, subject to the *de minimis* exemption where the child's income does not exceed £100, TA 1988, s 663(4). Where there is a court order directing a father to make payments directly to his child, the Inland Revenue does not regard these payments as creating a settlement. Under these circumstances, the child's income would not be aggregated with that of either parent.

The use of accumulation trusts is one way to create a settlement for the benefit of minor children. Where there is an irrevocable settlement of capital and the trustees are empowered or directed to accumulate the income arising from it for the ultimate benefit of the settlor's children, the settlor will not incur any income tax liability so long as the income is actually accumulated. The trust income is taxed at 35 per cent in the name of the trustees. If any sums are paid to or for the benefit of the child before his or her eighteenth birthday or earlier marriage, such sums will be treated as the settlor's income. When the accumulated income is paid to adult beneficiaries, it is normally treated as capital in their hands. See also Chapter 7 and below, regarding the favourable treatment of these trusts for IHT purposes.

All of the above provisions apply generally but where the settlor is either not domiciled, not resident, or not ordinarily resident in the United Kingdom, certain other considerations come into play. Under TA 1988, s 681(1), income arising under a settlement includes any income chargeable to income tax and any income which would have been so chargeable if it had been received in the United Kingdom by a person domiciled, resident and ordinarily resident in the United Kingdom. But where, in any year of assessment, the settlor is not resident, etc, in the United Kingdom then the settlement income in that year will not include any income which would not have been chargeable on the settlor, had he been entitled to it, by reason of his non-residence, etc.

The other consideration concerns settlements for the settlor's children. Where the settlor is not taxable as a UK resident then there is no aggregation. Any income from such a settlement paid to the child will not be treated as the parent's income for any year in which the parent is not resident in the United Kingdom. Under these circumstances, the child beneficiary will be able to reclaim the tax deducted on his income from the trust up to the amount of the single person's allowance. Where tax has been deducted at 35 per cent he will also be able to reclaim the 10 per cent additional rate tax on the income beyond his personal allowance.

8.5.5 Capital gains tax

Capital gains tax may become payable on the creation of a trust, on gains made in the trust, and on certain deemed disposals of trust assets. On the first of these the liability is likely to fall on the settlor, while on the second and third, the tax will be payable by the trustees out of the trust funds.

Whether a settlement is revocable or otherwise, a transfer into a settlement is considered to be a disposal of the entire property which becomes settled (TCGA 1992, s 70). This implies a deemed disposal by the transferor and the disposal will be treated as being made at market value. If this results in a capital gain then the transferor may elect to have the gain held over, if the asset consists of business assets (TCGA 1992, s 165) agricultural property (TCGA 1992, Sched 7) or where the transfer is chargeable to IHT (TCGA 1992, s 260). If the deemed disposal shows a loss then this loss may normally only be utilised by the transferor against subsequent gains arising in his transactions with the trust (TCGA 1992, s 18(3)). Gains may only be held over where the trustees are resident in the United Kingdom (TCGA 1992, ss 166, 261).

During the administration of a trust, gains and losses will accrue to the trustees as they would to an individual managing his portfolio. Net gains are chargeable at 25 per cent (or 35 per cent for a discretionary or accumulation settlement) subject to the restricted exemption mentioned earlier. In the case of trusts where the settlor or settlor's spouse could receive any benefit, the gains are aggregated with the settlor's to determine the rate of tax.

When property ceases to be settled property, if, for example, it is distributed or a person becomes absolutely entitled to it, that is a deemed disposal and an occasion of charge on any gain (TCGA 1992, s 71(1)). Where property ceases to be settled on the death of a life tenant, there is also a deemed disposal but there will be no chargeable gain (TCGA 1992, s 72). If the trustees and recipient of the disposed property agree and so elect, the gain accruing on property eligible for roll-over relief may be held over provided that the recipient is resident in the United Kingdom (TCGA 1992, Sched 7). Where a life interest in settled property comes to an end, there is no charge if the property remains within the settlement; there is no deemed disposal.

8.5.6   Inheritance tax

When a person creates a settlement there will be a diminution of the settlor's estate unless he settles the property on himself for life (IHTA 1984, s 3). This transfer of value may give rise to a liability for IHT. The IHT legislation treats differently settlements where there is or are interest(s) in possession, and those where there is no interest in possession.

Where a person is beneficially entitled to the interest in possession of settled property, he is treated as being beneficially entitled to the property in which the interest subsists (IHTA 1984, s 49(1)). Thus if two people had equal interests in possession of a trust worth £200,000, each would be treated as being entitled to £100,000. On the death of one of these persons IHT would be payable on the deemed transfer of £100,000 in addition to any other estate the deceased might have. Other events will also be treated as dispositions of the property by the person beneficially entitled to the interest in possession; if, for example, the interest is terminated during the life of the person or if it is disposed of by way of assignment or surrender. Where the disposal is for a consideration in money or money's worth, IHT will be charged on the value transferred less the consideration received.

There are, however, exceptions to this rule. If a person becomes absolutely entitled to the property or to another interest in possession, that will not be treated as a chargeable transfer (IHTA 1984, s 53(2)). Other exceptions include where the property reverts to the settlor or his spouse (if she, or he, is domiciled in the United Kingdom) or to the widow or widower of the settlor within two years of the death of the settlor (IHTA 1984, s 53(3)–(5)).

A reversionary interest is a future interest under a settlement. For IHT purposes, a reversionary interest is normally excluded property unless it was acquired at any time for money or money's worth (IHTA 1984, s 48(1)).

With one major exception, trusts where there is no interest in possession are treated harshly for IHT purposes. The major problem with the normal discretionary trust is the liability for the periodic charge under IHTA 1984, s 64. This charge is levied every tenth anniversary of the settlement date (falling after 31 March 1983) and is charged at 30 per cent of the rate which would be payable on a notional transfer of the value of the property in the trust at the end of the ten-year period. The rate is the lifetime rate of the settlor and is calculated on the settlor's previous chargeable transfers in the ten years preceding the creation of the settlement: IHTA 1984, ss 65 and 67. For further details, see the *Allied Dunbar Capital Taxes and Estate Planning Guide*.

Inheritance tax is also payable on other occasions when property is distributed from the trust to beneficiaries (including the settlor and his or her spouse) in anticipation of the ten-year charge (IHTA 1984, s 65).

The exception to this highly taxed regime is the accumulation and maintenance settlement. Such settlements are greatly favoured and narrowly defined by IHTA 1984, s 71. They are settlements where one or more beneficiaries will, upon attaining a specified age not exceeding 25, become entitled to an interest in possession in the settled property; no interest in possession subsists in the settled property and the income from the property is to be accumulated insofar as it is not applied for the maintenance, education, or benefit of a beneficiary; and either not more than 25 years have elapsed since the trust was created or became an accumulation and maintenance trust, or all the persons who are or have been beneficiaries are or were grandchildren of a common grandparent.

The commonest use of such trusts is along the following lines: S creates a settlement under which his children obtain an interest in possession at age 21 and at age 35, say, or upon earlier marriage, they receive the capital. Income up to age 21 is to be accumulated apart from any payments made for the beneficiaries' maintenance. No lifetime IHT is payable on transfers into accumulation trusts, on any maintenance payment made, on the beneficiaries' acquisition of the interest in possession, or on the release of capital and accumulated income (IHTA 1984, s 71(3)). Neither is there a periodic charge on these settlements (IHTA 1984, s 58(1)(*b*)). But one point to bear in mind if a payment is made for the benefit of the child under age 18 and unmarried, is that it will be treated as the income of the settlor if the settlor is the parent, under TA 1988, s 663.

Accumulation and maintenance settlements offer one of the most tax-efficient ways of transferring capital to children or grandchildren.

8.5.7 Non-resident trusts

Non-resident trusts may have a particular appeal to the expatriate who is used to having his investments sheltered from the Inland Revenue and who wishes to retain a similar advantage on his return either for himself or for the benefit of his children. There can certainly be advantages in setting up non-resident trusts but the anti-avoidance legislation is a real minefield for the unwary. It is essential to consider this legislation most carefully before opting to place substantial sums in what can be an expensive attempt to establish shelter and then finding that it does not achieve its main aim.

As mentioned earlier in this chapter, a trust settled by a UK-resident, ordinarily resident or domiciled settlor, will be treated as resident in the United Kingdom unless the general administration of the trust is carried on outside the United Kingdom and the trustees, or, for CGT purposes, a majority of them, are not resident or not ordinarily resident in the United Kingdom.

The UK income of a non-resident trust is liable to UK income tax at the basic rate and, so far as it is to be accumulated or is payable under a discretion, at the 10 per cent additional rate: see *IRC v Regent Trust Co Ltd* [1980] STC 140. It should be noted, however, that where the income has tax deducted at source or has an accompanying tax credit, the additional rate is charged only on the net income. For example, a non-UK resident trust receiving dividends of £750 (with tax credit of £250) would be liable for additional tax of £750 × 10 per cent=£75 leaving a net income of £675. A UK resident trust would have suffered total tax of £350 (tax credit of £250 plus £1,000 × 10 per cent) leaving a net £650.

From an income tax point of view, general principles can be applied which indicate that income paid to a beneficiary, where he is entitled to that income, will form part of his income for tax purposes. Where the trust is an accumulation trust, then accumulated income will not be taxable on the beneficiary and this may be paid to the beneficiary as capital in due course. General principles apart, there are several anti-avoidance provisions which also come into play.

The most important of these income tax provisions are contained in TA 1988, s 739–746. Section 739 is seen as one of the most widely drawn anti-avoidance provisions. Where an individual transfers assets so that someone not resident or domiciled in the United Kingdom receives any income from these assets, and that income can be used currently or at some future time by the individual who transferred the assets, then that income will be treated as income of the transferor.

What this means in the context of trusts is that if an individual, ordinarily resident in the United Kingdom, has established a non-resident trust under which he may benefit, then the income of the trust will be treated as his income whether or not it is distributed. It will be similarly taxed if the settlor's spouse may benefit. Section 739 will not apply while the settlor is not ordinarily resident, but a non-resident trust established during a period of non-residence will be caught when the expatriate returns to the United Kingdom. This section relates only to income and does not, therefore, operate to tax capital gains (see later). If income from or accruing to a non-resident trust is to escape UK income tax then the settlor and his or her spouse must be totally precluded from any possible benefit, and the words 'power to enjoy' are widely construed under TA 1988, s 742(2). Alternatively, if it can be shown that the trust was established for *bona fide* commercial reasons, such as the establishment of a pension scheme, and that the avoidance of tax was no part of this reasoning, the section will not operate (TA 1988, s 741). This will be very difficult to prove especially since exchange controls (once a useful commercial reason) no longer operate in the United Kingdom.

It should be noted that non-UK life assurance policies held in a non-resident trust are subject to UK tax on maturity under TA 1988, s 553(5).

On a more positive note, non-resident trusts can be established for the benefit of, for example, the settlor's children without any UK tax liability on the income as it arises overseas (see earlier for income arising in the United Kingdom). This is all well and good so long as the trust funds are accumulated. Unless the settlor and his spouse are excluded from benefit, TA 1988, s 674 can deem the trust income to be that of the settlor. Where there is a distribution of income that income becomes chargeable on the beneficiary under TA 1988, s 740 if he or she is ordinarily resident in the United Kingdom, Where a benefit is received under the trust, then that benefit will be taxed to the extent that the trust has relevant income. Where the benefit exceeds the relevant income then the excess will be taxed in later years as the trust accrues further relevant income. Relevant income is income of the trust which can be used to provide a benefit but is restricted to income which arose on or after 10 March 1981. If, for example, a non-resident trust established in 1975 accrued income at the rate of £2,000 a year, then in May 1988 the total income is £26,000 of which, say £14,000 is relevant income. During that year, £30,000 is paid to a beneficiary. The beneficiary's income tax liability in 1988/89 would be on £14,000 and, if income continues to accrue to the trust at the same rate, a further liability on £2,000 a year for the next eight years. If, however, the trust also had realised capital gains accrued since 10 March 1981, then to the extent that there is insufficient relevant income in the year of distribution, the surplus or a part of it will be allocated to the accrued capital gains and taxed accordingly.

In general terms, a non-resident trust established prior to 19 March 1991 by a UK domiciliary is not liable to UK CGT (except where it is carrying on a trade in the United Kingdom). However, where the settlor was domiciled and either resident or ordinarily resident in the United Kingdom when the trust was established, or in a relevant subsequent year when trust gains, or gains of companies owned by such trusts, TCGA 1992, s 97, are distributed to a UK domiciled beneficiary (FA 1981, s 80), those gains will be treated as accruing to the beneficiary and taxable on him. Gains of the trust are computed each year and the cumulative total of gains is treated as trust gains for the year. When a capital payment is made to beneficiaries, the trust gains will be attributed to them in proportion to the capital payment received by them up to the amount of that payment. Unattributed gains, ie where total gains are in excess of the capital payment, will be carried forward as trust gains for subsequent years. Gains are not apportioned to non-UK domiciled or non-UK resident beneficiaries. Tax on gains apportioned to a UK resident and domiciled beneficiary after 6 April 1992 may be increased by 10 per cent per annum as if it were interest for a maximum of six years (TCGA 1992, ss 91–97).

Trusts which emigrate from the United Kingdom on or after 19 March 1991 as a result of the appointment of non-resident trustees are deemed to have sold and re-acquired their assets at market value immediately before emigration, which could crystalise a CGT charge on exit (TCGA 1992, s 80) unless the emigration is caused by the death of a trustee and the trust is re-imported within six months (TCGA 1992, s 84). Past trustees may be made liable for the tax (TCGA 1992, s 82). Anti-avoidance provisions cover trusts benefiting from double taxation treaties, dual resident trusts and disposals of settled interests (TCGA 1992, ss 83–85). A UK domiciled settlor setting up a non-resident trust after 19 March 1991, or adding to an existing trust after that date, is taxed on the trust's capital gains as they arise if he or his spouse, child or child's spouse, or a company controlled by them, is a beneficiary (TCGA 1992, s 86 and Sched 5). This is under the provisions of TCGA 1992, ss 77–79, which assess the settlor of a UK trust who retains an interest.

As far as IHT is concerned, non-resident trusts are treated in very much the same way as resident trusts. The important point for the tax liability of these trusts is the domicile of the settlor at the time the trust is first established. If the settlor is not UK domiciled, then trust assets located outside the United Kingdom will be excluded from any IHT liability. The professional adviser has a duty to return details of any non-resident trusts established for a UK domiciled individual under IHTA 1984, s 218. Reference must be made, however, to any double taxation agreement in force. Where a non-resident trust has an IHT liability, this normally falls on the trustees but if, for whatever reason, the liability is not met by them, the Inland Revenue may obtain the tax from any of the following under IHTA 1984, s 201:

(1) any person entitled to an interest in possession in the settled property;
(2) any person for whose benefit the property or income therefrom may be applied at or after the time of the transfer; or
(3) the settlor, if the transfer is made within his lifetime.

In summary, non-resident trusts can be very useful in tax planning. Where the settlor and his or her spouse are precluded from income, the income payable to beneficiaries is effectively taxed on a remittance basis. The rules for capital gains are now rather complex, as summarised above, but do not affect non-domiciled settlors. Before embarking on any trust scheme, the expatriate must be totally clear on what he hopes to achieve and must be professionally advised in order to achieve it.

9 Other UK taxes

9.1 Value added tax

United Kingdom VAT is payable at the standard rate of 17.5 per cent in respect of goods or services supplied in the United Kingdom by a registered business. Registration is compulsory where the taxable turnover exceeds £36,600 a year. Certain items are exempt from VAT, while others are zero-rated, for example, most food. So far as the expatriate is concerned, the most important VAT relief is that relating to exports of goods or services. If goods are exported from the United Kingdom the sale is zero-rated, and therefore VAT should not be charged. Certain supplies of international services are also zero-rated; for example, an expatriate obtaining advice from a UK business, on his personal tax affairs, will receive a zero-rated bill if he is resident outside the EC. However, if he is resident inside the EC the charge will be standard-rated. A supply to the expatriate of taxation advice for business purposes is zero-rated whenever he is resident outside the United Kingdom.

Value added tax due on imports of goods is paid at the time and place of entry or, if the importer has approval for deferment, by direct debit covered by banker's guarantee on the fifteenth of the month following the month in which the goods enter the United Kingdom. However, from 1 January 1993, businesses which import goods from EC member states only account for VAT on their next VAT return.

9.1.1 VAT exemptions and zero-rating

The main VAT exemptions are set out in the Value Added Tax Act 1983 (VATA 1983), Sched 6: the main headings are land (but see **9.1.2**), insurance, finance, education, health, burial and cremation.

Zero-rating for VAT purposes is given by VATA 1983, Sched 5, the main headings of which are food, books, news services, fuel and power, construction of dwellings, international services (see below), transport, caravans and houseboats designed for permanent habitation, gold, medicines, certain supplies to or by charities and children's clothing.

International services include services relating to land outside the United Kingdom, letting goods for hire outside the United Kingdom, the supply of cultural, artistic, sporting, scientific, educational or entertainment services performed outside the United Kingdom, valuation of goods outside the United Kingdom, the supply to a person in his business capacity of services listed in VATA 1983, Sched 3 to a member of the EC and in any capacity to a person belonging elsewhere, and the supply of insurance and allied services and export and transshipment services. Goods sent to the United Kingdom for repair and subsequently re-exported are also included in this heading. Schedule 3 refers to services treated as supplied where received such as transfers and assignments of intellectual property, advertising services, professional services of consultants, engineers, lawyers, accountants, etc, banking, financial and insurance services, the supply of staff, hiring of goods and certain restrictive covenants.

If these services are supplied by a person who belongs outside the United Kingdom to a UK business registered for VAT, then the same consequences apply as if the recipient had himself supplied the services in the United Kingdom and that supply was a taxable supply, ie he would have to account for VAT on the value of that supply by the overseas person. Therefore if the UK business was partially exempt for UK VAT purposes, and these services received related to exempt supplies, it will suffer a disallowance of VAT input tax on these expenses. A UK business will therefore not obtain an advantage by using services supplied from abroad, which do not have a VAT charge on them, as opposed to services supplied in the United Kingdom which will bear VAT.

9.1.2 Property

Expatriates with property in the United Kingdom should appreciate that although the purchase price of domestic property is free of VAT, alterations as well as repairs and maintenance are subject to VAT. The construction of buildings for industrial and commercial use and in the community and civil engineering sector is standard rated for VAT: the landlord has the option to charge VAT on rents and capital sums received on the supply of non-domestic buildings and developed land used for non-domestic purposes. By electing for this, the landlord is able to recover input tax on repairs and maintenance expenses. Therefore expatriate owners of commercially let property in the United Kingdom should consider whether or not to register for UK VAT and appointing an agent in the United Kingdom to deal with their UK VAT affairs.

9.2   Car tax

Cars supplied in the United Kingdom other than for export are subject to a car tax in addition to VAT.

An expatriate returning to the United Kingdom and importing a car could be liable to both VAT and car tax on the value of the car at the time of importation, plus import duty if the car is not of EC origin (see below).

9.3   Excise duties

Many items imported into the United Kingdom suffer excise duties in addition to VAT. Examples include the obvious ones of alcohol and tobacco, perfume and gold and other less likely items such as cigarette lighters. Items acquired in the United Kingdom for personal export may be acquired in duty-free shops or those operating a personal export scheme under which the VAT, but not excise duty, may be recovered.

9.4   Personal belongings

The importation of personal belongings is normally subject to import duty, VAT and car tax (if relevant). The value for import duty is basically the secondhand value (exclusive of VAT) in the United Kingdom of identical or similar objects. The value for VAT is the same but inclusive of import duty. The value for car tax is the trade value inclusive of import duty but exclusive of VAT. (See Customs and Excise Notice 252.)

There are relieving provisions and these relate to three categories of belongings:

(1)   cars, aircraft and caravans,
(2)   boats, and
(3)   other effects.

The appropriate customs formalities including the claiming of the reliefs must be complied with:

(1) Motor cars, motor bikes, aircraft and mobile homes can be admitted entirely tax and duty free if belonging to a person coming into the United Kingdom for a stay of at least six months which are already his personal property and have been owned and used abroad by him or his spouse for six months excluding time he has spent in the United Kingdom. Furthermore, the vehicle must be for personal use and not sold, hired, etc for one year from importation under penalty of forfeiture. Release may be granted, if all duties and tax are paid. There is also a temporary importation relief for a visitor intending to stay less than six months in the United Kingdom, but the vehicle must be exported at the end of this period (see Customs and Excise Notice 3, and the Private Vehicle Memo).

(2) Boats are not in any case subject to import duty if more than 12 metres long. All boats designed or adapted for recreation or pleasure are subject to VAT as are other boats of less than 15 tons gross. The relieving provisions are virtually identical to those for motor cars (see Customs and Excise Notice 8A and later Customs and Excise Notice 8).

(3) Other baggage, personal and household effects (including pets) are relieved in the same way as cars, etc, except that these goods need only have been owned and used in the expatriate's normal home for three months if he is returning from the EC: the six month rule applies if he is returning from outside the EC and the goods are not disposed of for 12 months. These rules also apply to someone setting up a secondary home in the United Kingdom. Certain prohibited or restricted goods are not within this relief, eg, goods bought under a tax-free scheme. The normal duty-free allowances apply in addition to this relief (see Customs and Excise Notice 3).

(4) In addition to the above reliefs, a person who is resident outside the EC and who intends to become normally resident in the United Kingdom on the occasion of his marriage can bring in, duty and VAT free, wedding gifts up to a value of £700 each provided that they are from non-residents. Personal and household effects need not have been used abroad, but the goods should be imported within two months before, or four months after, the wedding.

9.5   Stamp duty

Stamp duty on the conveyance of UK stocks and shares is chargeable at $\frac{1}{2}$ per cent. In the case of property the charge is 1 per cent or nil if the value transferred is £30,000 or less. Stamp duty on gifts is 50p.

Of particular interest to expatriates is the stamp duty provision under which a stampable document signed outside the United Kingdom and kept outside the United Kingdom is only stampable within 30 days of being brought into the United Kingdom (Stamp Act 1891, s 15(2)(*a*)).

10 The taxpayer's rights and obligations in his country of residence*

Whatever the expatriate's position in his present country of residence, whether, that is to say, he is living in retirement, in full-time employment, or self-employed, he will be well advised to have a clear idea of his basic rights and obligations *vis-à-vis* the local tax administration. Although in many countries these rights and obligations will be similar to those in force in the United Kingdom, the expatriate is likelier to find himself in a situation calling for some knowledge of them than he would have been if he had never left his native shores. It can be dangerous, in other words, for the expatriate to take anything for granted as far as his host country's tax system is concerned. To give a specific example of the kind of thing the expatriate needs to be aware of, many countries require a person leaving after a stay of several months or more to have a clearance certificate from their tax authorities before he is allowed to go. Again, some countries levy local taxes without sending any notification directly to the taxpayer concerned: it is up to the taxpayer to find out from some official publication or other that a tax payment is due from him.

10.1 Taxpayers' rights

Insistence on the political rights of taxpayers first appears in history in the 18th century. 'Taxation without representation is tyranny' was a watchword of the American Revolution, and Art 14 of the 1789 French Declaration of Human Rights laid it down that citizens have the right to decide themselves, or through their representatives, on the necessity for public contributions and the

*This chapter is based on the OECD publication *Taxpayers' Rights and Obligations: A survey of the legal situation in OECD countries*, Paris, 1990

use to which they should be put, and to determine the amount, base and duration of such levies. Article 14 also states that citizens should have an obligation to pay these taxes.

In the modern world, democratic governments at least take the political rights of taxpayers for granted. In this chapter we are concerned rather with what might be termed administrative rights, the rights, in other words, that govern the individual taxpayer's actual dealings with the tax authorities. We are also concerned primarily with income tax. There is no international convention on such rights, but in many countries there is a growing awareness on the part of government that taxpayers need more explicit and comprehensive provisions to protect their rights at a time when tax levels are high, tax legislation grows more complex from year to year, and new technology is both making it easier in principle for information from different sources to be exchanged and checked, and allowing more co-operation between tax authorities in different jurisdictions.

The 25 member states of the Organisation for Economic Cooperation and Development all recognise, whether implicitly or explicitly, the following basic principles of taxpayer protection.

10.1.1   Right to be informed, assisted and heard

Taxpayers are entitled to have up-to-date information on the operation of the tax system, with its complexity duly reflected, and the way in which their tax is assessed. They are also entitled to be informed of their rights, including their rights of appeal.

10.1.2   Right of appeal

The right to appeal against any decision of the tax authorities applies to all taxpayers, and to almost all decisions taken by the tax authorities, whether as regards the application and interpretation of the law or of administrative rulings, provided the taxpayer is directly concerned.

10.1.3   Right to pay no more than the correct amount of tax

Taxpayers should pay no more tax than is required by the tax legislation, taking into account their personal circumstances and income. The tax authorities, however, and whatever tribunals or courts may be concerned try to make a distinction between legitimate tax planning and forms of tax avoidance or minimisation that can be proved to go against the intention of the legislators. Taxpayers are also entitled to a reasonable measure of assistance from the tax authorities so that they receive all the reliefs and deductions to which they are entitled; but in many countries tax reliefs are not automatically given even if all the information is available to the authorities.

10.1.4   Right to certainty

Taxpayers have the right to a high degree of certainty as to the tax consequences of their actions. A related point is that legislation and changes in the administrative interpretation of tax laws should not normally be retroactive.

10.1.5   Privacy

All taxpayers have the right to expect that the tax authorities will not intrude unnecessarily upon their privacy. In practice, this is interpreted as avoiding unreasonable searches of their homes and requests for information which is not relevant for determining the correct amount of tax due.

10.1.6   Confidentiality and secrecy

The information available to the tax authorities on the affairs of the taxpayer is confidential and will be used only for the purposes specified in the tax legislation.

With regard to exchanges of information between tax administrations in different countries, requests may be refused if the requested authority believes there is a risk of disclosure. Some countries require the tax authorities to inform the taxpayer before any information is passed to another government department or foreign tax authority.

In the majority of OECD member countries the tax administration has the statutory power to override bank secrecy and to obtain specific information from the bank for tax purposes, although this power is normally used with reserve and not unless there is some serious matter at issue. The rules and practice on this score, however, vary considerably from one country to another.

10.2   Taxpayers' obligations

Taxpayers also have certain **obligations** enforceable by law, the chief of which, administratively speaking, is to file an annual return. This often has to be done within a specified deadline, with a penalty for failure to comply. In many countries taxpayers must supply additional information or specified documentation on the request of the authorities. In some countries there is a specific legal obligation to report on a change in the taxpayer's situation, such as the formation of a partnership, initiation of some professional activity, or acquisition of a new source of income.

Further details about taxpayers' obligations in OECD member countries and the consequences if the requirements of the tax authorities are not met are set out in the following table.

Table 10.1 Taxpayers' obligations

Country	Obligations to make annual return	Population receiving tax returns	Other obligations	Consequences if requirements are not met
Australia	All taxpayers are legally obliged to file a return following a notice requiring filing signed by the Commissioner.	All taxable persons and companies (except taxpayers with income mainly from employment) who filed a form in the preceding year.	Upon notice from the Commissioner taxpayers must furnish necessary information, attend and give evidence, produce books and documentation, furnish special returns, keep business records if certain deductions are claimed and records of acquisitions and disposal of assets owned since 19 September 1985.	Assessment by Commissioner, penalty of double the amount of tax assessed can be imposed, prosecution and penalties of up to $2,000 (1st offence), $4,000 (2nd offence), $5,000 or up to 12 months imprisonment (3rd offence) plus additional measures.
Austria	Follows from the respective tax laws or from a specific request issued by the tax office.	Taxpayers with income subject to assessment with certain limitations (does not cover employment which is subject to withholding tax).	Taxpayers obliged to notify to the tax office all relevant facts or circumstances relevant for existence or scope of tax liability.	Administrative fines (max Sch 20,000) and/or penal proceedings. Delays can be punished by surcharge up to 10% of assessed tax.

(continues)

Country	Obligations to make annual return	Population receiving tax returns	Other obligations	Consequences if requirements are not met
Belgium	All taxpayers (except individuals with low income) must file an annual return.	Persons and corporations receiving taxable income.	The tax administration has at its disposal rights to obtain certain supplementary information from taxpayers.	Assessment by tax office, increase of assessed tax between 10 and 200%, administrative penalties (BF200–10,000) or legal prosecutions.
Canada	All corporations (except charity) and all individuals with tax payable must file a return.	All corporations and individuals who filed a return in the previous year.	To take advantage of certain special provisions in the Income Tax Act a special form must be filed.	Failure to file returns in time results in penalty equal to 5% of unpaid tax plus up to 1% of unpaid tax per month (maximum 12 months).
Denmark	All taxpayers are legally obliged to file an annual return.	All taxable persons and corporations.	On request taxpayers must supply information, eg, documentation for deducted expenses.	Assessment made by tax authorities.
Finland	All taxpayers (except non-residents paying final withholding tax at source) must file a return.	Residents who received income in the previous year.	Specific rules for non-resident taxpayers.	Increased tax depending on degree of negligence.

France	All taxpayers are legally obliged to file a return.	All taxable persons and corporations.	Taxpayers must supply supplementary information on certain tax allowances.	After the order of tax authority is given, assessment interest of 0.75 per cent per month, tax increase of 10, 40 or 80%, allowance may not be accepted if no documentation is supplied.
Germany	All persons subject to taxation with the exception of certain employed persons subject to withholding tax on wages.	All known taxpayers with the exception of employed persons with final tax payments by withholding tax on wages.	Authorities must be notified of the setting up of corporations and partnerships, agricultural and forestry undertakings, business enterprises and self-employment as well as of certain direct investments abroad and the manufacture of excisable goods.	Estimation of income and supplementary charges.

(continues)

Country	Obligations to make annual return	Population receiving tax returns	Other obligations	Consequences if requirements are not met
Greece	All natural persons with taxable income earned. All legal entities.	All individuals having filed a tax return in previous years.	Individuals and companies must notify the tax office of changes in their situation, eg, commencement, interruption of business, legal modifications of the company, the value of own stocks, various contracts of construction of buildings, etc.	Failure to file returns in time or accurately results in a fine. Fine differs in kinds of cases, but without considering intention to evade taxes.
Ireland	All persons liable to tax by Direct Assessment and all other persons who are required to do so by a notice from the tax inspector.	Employed taxpayers liable to income tax and pay related social insurance by deduction at source through the PAYE system (with allowances other than basic) plus full issue of returns to taxpayers liable to tax by direct assessment.	Persons and corporations must on request supply additional information on accounts, books and documents and assets. Chargeable persons who have not been required to do so must file a return and new companies must furnish basic data on the company.	Administrative assessment of taxable income, penalties and – if failure is wilful – additional penalties.

Italy	All persons with income (varies by source of income) above a certain level are required to file a return.	All taxable persons and corporations.	Taxpayer must supply supplementary information on request.	Prosecution, imprisonment (up to 5 years) and fine (amount varies).
Japan	Each taxpayer must assess his own income tax and file a return.	All persons estimated to be liable to file a final return.	Persons receiving gross income of more than Y30 million from business shall submit special report unless final return submitted.	No penalty.
Netherlands	All taxpayers are legally obliged to file a return.	Persons who are suspected to be liable to tax or required to withhold tax.	Taxpayers must supply relevent documents. Legal entities must submit a list of directors.	Assessment on an estimated basis by tax inspector, in some instances with a surcharge of 5% or a criminal fine up to GLD 10,000. In criminal cases up to 4 years imprisonment and/or fines up to GLD 25,000. In cases of re-assessment or additional assessment a surcharge of 100% may be imposed on tax levied.

(continues)

Country	Obligations to make annual return	Population receiving tax returns	Other obligations	Consequences if requirements are not met
New Zealand	All persons with assessable income except employees subject to withholding tax with earnings less than certified amount.	Every person with an IRD identification number and for whom a current address is held.	Details of payments made to non-residents (eg dividends, interest) subject to non-resident withholding tax, information on all interest paid or credited in the course of business and information from employers on payments or benefits made or given to employees.	Prosecution and fines up to $6,000.
Norway	All persons and companies with income or capital taxable in Norway must file a return, except certain categories of pension recipients.	All persons and companies with assessed income in the previous year plus those who inform authorities that they will have taxable income.	Taxpayers operating business enterprises must supply additional information (annual balance of accounts).	Taxpayer can lose right of administrative appeal, authorities can make discretionary assessment, or an additional penalty can be imposed.
Portugal	All persons with an income above certain limits and all companies.	No tax return is sent to taxpayers.	Taxpayers subject to corporate tax are required to provide some	Fines of varying size assessment by inspector and interest on tax due.

Spain	All taxpayers, and individuals who have taxable income greater than Ptas 840,000.	Tax returns are not sent to taxpayers.	additional information (eg depreciation, expenses, royalties, etc). Taxpayers are required to report to the authority on initiation and termination of their business or professional activities, as well as on change in their fiscal domicile.	Fines are imposed. After a tax audit, taxpayers are punished with withdrawal of tax reliefs, in certain cases by legal prosecution.
Sweden	All persons with an income of at least SKr 10,000 (with certain exceptions), except certain categories of pension recipients plus nearly all corporations.	All filers for previous year plus — according to information held — persons obliged to file a return for year in question.	All taxpayers are obliged to furnish any piece of information necessary for a correct assessment (normally submitted together with tax return).	Administrative fines, administrative assessment, combined with increase in tax, legal prosecution.
Switzerland	All taxpayers must file a tax return.	All taxpayers.	Obligation to furnish information on the request of tax administration.	Administrative assessment, administrative fines or legal prosecution.

(*continues*)

Country	Obligations to make annual return	Population receiving tax returns	Other obligations	Consequences if requirements are not met
Turkey	All persons and corporations with income subject to tax (with certain exceptions).	Tax returns are not sent to taxpayers.	Taxpayers or other related persons and public institutions must furnish all necessary information to tax authorities.	Special penalties (up to TL 240,000).
United Kingdom	Only taxpayers receiving a return from the inspector.	All taxpayers with income subject to assessment, but only approx. one-sixth of taxpayers with income mainly from employment.	Any new source of income must be notified.	Penalties of up to 100% of the tax due.
United States	All taxpayers are in principle obliged to file a return (exceptions being some persons with gross income below a certain limit).	Persons who filed a form the preceding year.	Taxpayers are required to pay estimated tax in instalments during the taxable year. Reporting is required in special cases (eg, US residents having interests in a foreign corporation or in a foreign financial	Fines of 5% of tax for a late return and 5% for each month late up to 25%. Fines of 20% of underpayment for certain failures to file an accurate return. Fines equal to the amount of interest on

account). Payments of certain income to non-resident alien individuals, foreign corporations, and foreign partners are subject to reporting and withholding tax.

underpayments of estimated tax instalments. Special fines concerning information on foreign corporations. (Persons required to deduct and withhold tax on income to a foreign person are liable for the tax.)

Source: *Taxpayers' Rights and Obligations, A survey of the legal situation in OECD countries*, Paris, 1990

11 Double taxation agreements

11.1 Fiscal residence

The United Kingdom taxes the worldwide income of a UK resident and domiciled individual and it also taxes the income arising in the United Kingdom of a non-resident. It will be appreciated that as many other countries do likewise, it is possible to be subject to tax on overseas income both in the country of residence and in the country in which the income arises. In many cases this problem is alleviated by a bilateral double taxation agreement between the two countries involved.

The United Kingdom currently has more than 90 double taxation agreements, some of which relate only to particular types of income. This book is aimed at the British expatriate, and it is therefore necessary to consider in the case of income arising in the United Kingdom whether there is a double tax treaty between the United Kingdom and the taxpayer's country of residence or not. If there is such a treaty, it is then necessary to consider the taxpayer's fiscal residence under the treaty.

Consider for example the case of the expatriate who has retired to Spain, where he spends the majority of the winter, but who has retained his house in the United Kingdom where he spends the summer months. Article 4 of the Anglo-Spanish Double Tax Treaty provides that it is necessary first of all to consider residence according to the rules of the country concerned. Under UK law, because of maintaining a place of abode in the United Kingdom, he is resident in any fiscal year in which he sets foot in the United Kingdom, as he does not have a full-time employment in Spain. As he spends some nine months of the year in Spain, he is resident in Spain for Spanish tax purposes.

It is then necessary to consider in which country he has a permanent home available to him. As he has a home in both countries, it is then necessary to consider his centre of vital interests — ie the state with which his personal and economic relations are closer. This is debatable. He spends three-quarters of his time in Spain but has by no means severed his ties with the United Kingdom. If the country in which he has his centre of vital interests cannot be determined, it is necessary to look to the country in which he has an habitual abode. But as he has such an abode in both countries it is then necessary to look to his nationality. If he is a UK national, he will be regarded as resident in the United Kingdom and non-resident in Spain and taxed accordingly. If he is a Spanish national, however, on the same facts he would be regarded as resident in Spain and not resident in the United Kingdom. If he is a national in neither the United Kingdom nor Spain, the tax authorities in each country will agree his place of residence. In the circumstances envisaged this would probably be Spain and he would therefore be regarded as not resident in the United Kingdom, notwithstanding the fact that he has a home here which would normally make him resident under the UK residence rules.

A number of the older treaties do not have this tiebreaker clause with regard to residence and it is therefore possible to be resident in both countries. This also applies where there is no double tax treaty. In this case, the tax liability must be calculated in accordance with the rules of each country and advantage taken of any remaining relief under the treaties and unilateral relief where available.

Exceptionally, the second protocol to the Anglo-US treaty (SI 1980 No 568) provides that for income tax purposes a woman with US citizenship who married a UK domiciled man before 1 January 1974 and therefore acquired a UK domicile of dependence is deemed to have married on that date and may therefore retain her US domicile of origin unless she acquires a UK domicile by choice.

11.2 Dividends

A non-resident in receipt of dividends from the United Kingdom is not entitled to the tax credit that is available to a UK resident unless the appropriate treaty so provides. The treaty with Spain for example provides in Art 10, para 3 that a Spanish resident entitled to dividends from a UK company is entitled to the same tax credit as a UK resident and is subject to Spanish tax on the gross equivalent of the dividends. However, the UK authorities subject the dividend to a withholding tax of 15 per cent on the gross equivalent and this tax is allowed as a credit against the Spanish tax payable. If therefore a British company paid a dividend of £75, the resident in Spain would receive £75 from the company and the UK Inland Revenue would repay the difference between the tax credit available to a UK resident of £25 and 15 per cent on the gross equivalent: that is £10. He would therefore receive £85 from the United Kingdom and would be regarded in Spain as having received dividends of £100 on which tax of £15 had already been paid.

If he were a resident of a non-treaty country, he would be treated as receiving income of £75 and would pay such local tax on that income as would be levied by the country of residence.

To avoid having to apply to the UK Inland Revenue for the repayment of part of the tax credit, it is possible to arrange for the company paying the dividend to repay the appropriate part of the tax credit at the same time. This requires the consent of the company and of the Inland Revenue under the Double Taxation Relief (Taxes on Income) (General) (Dividend) Regulations, SI 1973 No 317. (Usually known as the G arrangement.)

11.3 Interest

Interest arising in the United Kingdom to a non-resident is normally taxable in the United Kingdom under Schedule D, Case III, under TA 1988, s 18(3). There is an exception in the case of bank or building society interest paid direct to a non-resident which is not subject to UK tax in view of Extra-Statutory Concession B13 (1992). Annual interest, that is, on a loan exceeding 12 months, paid to a person whose usual place of abode is outside the United Kingdom, is subject to deduction of tax at the basic rate at source under TA 1988, s 349(2)(c) unless it is bank or building society interest. A non-resident can arrange that such interest is paid gross, see **4.3**.

Interest paid to a non-resident may suffer a reduced rate of withholding tax or be liable in the United Kingdom for a reduced rate of tax under the treaty. Article 11 of the Anglo-Spanish Treaty, for example, reduces the tax in the country where the interest arises to 12 per cent which would be credited against the liability in the country of residence. It is possible to arrange with the Inspector of Foreign Dividends to deduct tax at the reduced treaty rate, if any, on payment of interest to a non-resident under the Double Taxation Relief (Taxes on Income) (General) Regulations, SI 1970 No 488. This applies to both interest and royalties.

11.4   Royalties

Royalties paid from the United Kingdom to a non-resident are subject to a withholding tax at the basic rate of 25 per cent if they are royalties in respect of a UK patent under TA 1988, s 348(2) or in respect of copyright, and are paid to the owner of copyright whose usual place of abode is not within the United Kingdom under TA 1988, s 536. This section refers to a usual place of abode outside the United Kingdom, not residence outside the United Kingdom, although for practical purposes this will normally be the same. It should also be noted that copyright royalties paid to an author whose normal place of abode is outside the United Kingdom are not subject to withholding tax under TA 1988, s 536 in view of a Parliamentary Answer of 10 November 1969 (*Hansard* Vol 791, col 31).

Other royalties arising in the United Kingdom are not subject to withholding tax unless they are pure income profit where the non-resident provides no services whatsoever for the royalty received. If it is pure income profit, the tax would be withheld at source at the basic rate in the same way as for any other annual payment. Under the appropriate double tax treaty, it may be possible to reduce the rate of withholding tax and in the treaty with Spain, for example, the rate of withholding tax on royalties is reduced to 10 per cent by Art 12 of the treaty. As for interest, permission may be obtained from the Inspector of Foreign Dividends to pay the interest subject to this reduced rate of withholding tax.

11.5   Income from real property

Income from immovable property is normally taxed in the country in which it is situated, as under Art 6 of the Anglo-Spanish Double Tax Treaty. Income from property in the United Kingdom is subject to withholding tax under TA 1988, s 43 at the basic rate of tax where payment is made to a non-resident, although it is possible to arrange with the Inland Revenue for payment to be made subject to a reduced or nil level of withholding tax if it can be shown that the income arising will be reduced for UK tax purposes by, for example, mortgage interest paid.

11.6   Businesses

Business profits are normally only taxed in the country of residence unless there is a permanent establishment in the other country, see, for example, Art 7 of the Anglo-Spanish Double Tax Treaty. Permanent establishment is very often defined by the treaty, for example, in Art 5 of the double tax treaty with Spain, and includes a place of management, branch, office, factory, workshop, mine, oil well, etc, and in the case of Spain, a building site which exists for more than 12 months.

If there is a permanent establishment of a non-resident in the United Kingdom, it will be subject to UK tax on the profits. The assessment may be made in the name of an agent in the United Kingdom who is made responsible for the tax under TMA 1970, s 83, and who may withhold UK tax when accounting to his non-resident principal. A non-resident trading with the United Kingdom is not, under general law, subject to UK tax and it is specifically provided that a non-resident trading in the United Kingdom through a broker who is a general commission agent is not liable to UK tax in view of TMA 1970, s 82. If he is otherwise trading in the United Kingdom but not through a permanent establishment the treaty will normally protect him from UK tax. In the case of a business being carried on by a non-resident it is common for the treaty to reinforce the transfer pricing provisions of TA 1988, s 770 to ensure arm's length pricing between the United Kingdom and overseas business and in the case of Spain this is contained in Art 9 of the treaty.

11.7   Capital gains

A non-resident is not normally liable to UK CGT except in the case of assets used for a branch or business in the United Kingdom under TCGA 1992, s 10. Article 13 of the Anglo-Spanish Double Tax Treaty would allow the United Kingdom to tax immovable property in the United Kingdom, although in fact it does not do so, except for development gains under TA 1988, s 776.

11.8   Independent personal services

The self-employed activities of a non-resident will not normally be subject to tax in the United Kingdom unless there is a fixed base in the United Kingdom, as under Art 14 of the Anglo-Spanish treaty.

11.9 Dependent personal services

Employment income of a non-resident from activities in the United Kingdom would normally be taxable under Schedule E, Case II although this liability may be reduced by treaty relief. For example, under Art 15 of the Anglo-Spanish treaty, if the employer is not resident in the United Kingdom and the non-resident employee is present for a period not exceeding 183 days in the fiscal year, he would not be liable to UK tax under Schedule E, Case II for his work in the United Kingdom. On the other hand, directors' fees from a UK company would be subject to tax in the United Kingdom, in the case of Spain under Art 16 of the treaty.

11.10 Artistes and athletes

There are often special provisions relating to the remuneration of non-resident artistes and athletes whose remuneration may be very large. The treaty will usually provide that they are taxable in the country in which the performance is given even though they would otherwise be protected by the treaty, see, for example, Art 17 of the Anglo-Spanish treaty. Withholding tax at the basic rate from the UK earnings of non-UK resident artistes and athletes.

11.11 Students and teachers

There are often special provisions in double tax treaties relating to students and teachers. For example in the treaty with Spain, Art 20 provides that a previous resident of Spain who comes to the United Kingdom for training and who receives money for his maintenance, education or benefit is not taxable in the United Kingdom. This is obviously useful where the children of expatriates come back to the United Kingdom for the purposes of their education. Teachers, as in Art 21 of the Anglo-Spanish treaty, are often allowed a two-year period, in total, *IRC v Vas* [1990] STC 137, in another country without becoming liable to tax therein.

11.12 Pensions

Under most of the double taxation agreements that the United Kingdom has with other countries, pensions are normally only taxable in the country of residence. The exception is pensions which result from Government Service; these are normally taxable only in the country from which the pension originates unless paid to a national of the country of residence. For example, under the Anglo-Spanish treaty, a UK pension paid to a resident of Spain would be liable for tax only in Spain, by virtue of Art 18. However, if the pension resulted from service with HM Government or a local authority, it would be taxable only in the United Kingdom under Art 19(3), unless the recipient was a Spanish national in which case it would be taxable only in Spain.

Clearly the operation of the agreement is straightforward where the pension is paid gross — one simply makes the return to the appropriate authority. Where the pension is normally subject to deduction of tax at source, obtaining treaty relief is a little more involved. (Those pensions subject to tax deduction at source were outlined in Chapter 4 but briefly, they are likely to be any pension other than State pensions — Old Age Pension and State Earnings Related Pension — which are paid gross.) Authority for pension or retirement annuity payments to be made gross is granted by the:

> Inspector of Foreign Dividends
> Lynwood Road
> Thames Ditton, Surrey
> England KT7 0DP

The Inspector will grant permission on receipt of confirmation that the individual in question is resident for tax purposes in the other jurisdiction. There is an official confirmation form for each country with which the United Kingdom has a double taxation agreement — the form may be obtained from either tax authority and is printed in both languages. For instance, in the case of a resident of Spain Form SPA may be obtained from the Inspector of Foreign Dividends or from the local office of the *Delegación de Hacienda del domicilio fiscal del residente de España.*

11.12.1   UK State Retirement (Old Age) Pension

This is always paid gross to the recipient wherever resident and would normally be taxable in the country of residence.

11.12.2   Occupational pensions in respect of government or local authority service

These pensions, for example of civil servants, members of the armed services, state system school teachers etc would be paid subject to deduction of tax under PAYE at the appropriate code number. If the recipient is living in a treaty country it is unlikely that there would be a local tax liability in the country of residence on this income.

11.12.3 Occupational pensions (not government)

Occupational Pensions would normally be subject to deduction of tax under PAYE. A non-resident should be able to arrange for a no tax notice of coding from his local district, if he still submits UK income tax returns, or from the Inspector of Foreign Dividends. Such pensions will normally be taxable in the country of residence.

11.12.4 Self-employed pensions

Deferred annuities are normally subject to deduction of tax at the basic rate although a non-resident should be able to obtain the appropriate authority from the Inspector of Foreign Dividends for the annuity to be paid gross. Such income would normally be taxable in the country of residence.

11.13 Other income

In some treaties there is an article which provides that any other income arising in the treaty country will only be taxed in the country of residence. This article could, for example, apply to maintenance payments from the United Kingdom to a non-resident who would therefore receive the income gross or be able to recover the tax from the Inland Revenue. In the treaty with Spain 'other income' is in Art 22.

11.14 Non-discrimination

Treaties often contain what is known as a non-discrimination article which says generally that a non-resident shall not be treated worse than a resident for tax purposes. In the Anglo-Spanish treaty this is contained in Art 25. Non-discrimination clauses are very often more useful as a negotiating tool than for actual invocation.

11.15 Mutual agreement procedure

Most treaties also contain a mutual agreement procedure whereby a resident may ask his own tax authority to negotiate with the overseas tax authority if he considers that he is being unfairly treated, or the double taxation treaty is being ignored or misinterpreted. The mutual agreement procedure is, for example, often invoked or threatened to be invoked in negotiating with the Internal Revenue Service in the United States, who tend to have a somewhat cavalier view of the application of double tax treaties with other countries.

11.16   Exchange of information

One of the points to watch in living in a country where there is a double tax treaty with the United Kingdom, is that the treaty will usually contain a clause overriding the normal secrecy provisions and allow the appropriate tax authorities to exchange information relating to the taxpayer's financial affairs. Inland Revenue information gathering powers may now be used on behalf of other tax authorities within the European Community (FA 1990, s 125).

Although most treaties are similar in many respects, it is extremely important to refer to the actual treaty currently in force when considering the likely taxation charge as there are significant differences.

11.17   Inheritance tax

The United Kingdom has only ten double taxation treaties covering IHT and consequently they are generally of not so much importance as the income tax treaties. The countries with which agreements have been concluded are:

France	Republic of Ireland
India	Republic of South Africa
Italy	Sweden
Netherlands	Switzerland
Pakistan	United States

In some circumstances the treaties can change the fiscal domicile of an individual for IHT purposes which would obviously be of extreme importance in determining his UK IHT liability. For instance, under Art 4 of the IHT Double Taxation Treaty with South Africa, a South African national with a UK domicile who had not been ordinarily resident in the United Kingdom for seven years would be regarded as domiciled in South Africa and not in the United Kingdom. This seemingly arcane illustration is mirrored in other ways in other treaties and must serve as an example of the need to seek professional advice in situations where an individual is living in one jurisdiction and has assets in another.

Where two countries both have a claim to the same assets (for IHT purposes) the potential exists, despite the treaty, for double taxation to occur. For this reason most treaties contain a double taxation relief clause which will remove or, at the least, mitigate the double liability. Where there is no double taxation treaty between countries, unilateral relief against double taxation may be available whereby a credit for the overseas tax paid will be set against the UK IHT liability. The provisions are somewhat complex and are contained in IHTA 1984, s 159.

11.18   Unilateral relief

Double taxation relief is often given unilaterally where there is no treaty or the treaty does not cover the income in question. A UK resident is given unilateral relief under TA 1988, s 790. Unilateral relief will normally give credit for direct overseas taxes suffered but, for example, would not normally give an individual relief for the underlying taxes on a company's profits out of which a dividend is subsequently declared. As far as possible relief is given as if there had been a double taxation treaty in force, see SP 7/91.

11.19   Treaty shopping

In certain cases, it is possible to use a third country's double taxation agreement to reduce a withholding tax. For example, UK patent royalties paid from the United Kingdom to a resident of Hong Kong would normally suffer UK tax at 25 per cent. If, however, a Netherlands company were interposed, the UK royalties would be paid gross to the Netherlands under the UK-Netherlands Double Tax Treaty and 7 per cent or so of the royalties would remain in the Netherlands subject to Netherlands tax at 42 per cent. The remaining 93 per cent would, however, be paid on to Hong Kong free of withholding tax as the Netherlands does not levy a withholding tax on royalties.

This could not however be done for dividends from the United Kingdom as there is a specific anti-avoidance provision in the UK-

Netherlands treaty to prevent the use of the treaty by a third country resident.

Care is required, however, because, as in all tax matters, if there is first, a pre-ordained series of transactions and second, steps inserted which have no business *purpose* apart from avoidance of tax, the inserted steps will be ignored for tax purposes: see *Craven v White*, [1988] STC 476.

12 The returning expatriate

The successful handling of an expatriate's financial affairs requires careful planning before he leaves the United Kingdom, continuous awareness of the taxation consequences of his actions while overseas, and, perhaps most important of all, careful planning and sound advice before his return home. It would, after all, be rather unfortunate to have spent many years building up a substantial amount of capital only to have a large slice of it taken by the Inland Revenue through a lack of foresight on return. Fortunately, much can be done to mitigate potential tax charges, but it is essential for these mitigating devices to be put in train before the expatriate comes back to the United Kingdom. Effective tax planning the day after return will, more often than not, prove to be impossible or, at least, illegal or ineffective.

This chapter, in common with the rest of the book, is concerned primarily with taxation and investment, but the returning expatriate has more to consider than this, and an indication of some of the other areas of concern is also provided.

12.1 Tax liabilities on return

As already mentioned, the main determinant of a person's liability to UK income tax or CGT, apart, that is, from having an income or a capital gain, is his tax residence position. The mere ending of an overseas employment or a visit to the United Kingdom need not result in a change of residence. The change from non-resident to resident will only come about if any of the following circumstances apply:

(1) the person returns to the United Kingdom intending to remain permanently or for a number of years; or
(2) he spends 183 days or more in the United Kingdom in any particular tax year; or

(3) he visits the United Kingdom regularly for periods which average 90 or more days each year over a period of four consecutive tax years; or

(4) he pays any visit to the United Kingdom, no matter how brief, while not in full-time employment or self-employment overseas and when he has accommodation available for his use in the United Kingdom.

For the majority of returning expatriates, the first condition above will apply. But before going on to review the consequences of this, it is worth considering the not uncommon situation of the expatriate who returns home for a period, perhaps at the end of a contract, but with the intention of finding another overseas job at the earliest opportunity. A person in these circumstances need not become resident in the United Kingdom, but many do under the second or fourth condition above. Unlike the majority, this temporary resident will not become resident and ordinarily resident from the date of arrival: rather, he will become resident but not ordinarily resident for that year. The tax consequences here are quite different from those pertaining to the new permanent resident.

12.1.1 Taxation on remittance basis

An individual who is resident but not ordinarily resident will be taxed on the remittance basis, that is, on the income he actually brings into the United Kingdom. In some respects this can be a more onerous burden than that of the permanent resident. Income which arises in the United Kingdom will be wholly taxable; overseas investment income will be assessed on the remittances made during the preceding tax year (or the current year if the income source is new) as will any remittances from an overseas trade or profession.

The remittance of earnings arising in the year of return from overseas employment will also be taxable in the year of return, as will earnings arising in previous years from a trade within Schedule D. This latter liability is one of the major differences between the treatment of those who become ordinarily resident and those who do not. Taxable remittances can be in cash or kind, or they can be constructive remittances arising through various debt arrangements and similar devices. An expatriate who is likely to find himself in this position would be well advised to seek professional assistance at an early date, before his return, because the degree of tax liability will be determined by many individual factors which are beyond the scope of a general treatment here.

So far as CGT is concerned, an individual resident but not ordinarily resident will be fully liable on any gains made worldwide unless he is not domiciled in the United Kingdom. In the case of the non-domiciled individual he will be liable in full for gains made in the United Kingdom and on any gain remitted to the United Kingdom which arose abroad.

12.1.2 Tax on worldwide income

Returning to the majority case, the erstwhile expatriate will become resident and ordinarily resident from the day of his return. From then on, he will be fully liable to UK taxes on his worldwide income and capital gains. There are, however, one or two important exceptions and adjustments to this general rule. The first of these concerns any earnings from the overseas employment. Because, by concession, the tax year is split in the year of return into a resident and non-resident part, the overseas earnings before return escape tax. Subsequent payments including terminal leave pay, bonuses, gratuities, or lump sums from provident funds or in commutation of pension rights, used to be allowed tax free where they related to the overseas employment, but cease to be from 6 April 1992, under SP 18/91. Any pension which arises overseas and which is payable by reason of overseas employment is taxable in the United Kingdom (whether remitted or not) but 10 per cent of the amount received is exempted from tax under TA 1988, s 196.

Where the returned expatriate has a continuing source of overseas investment income this, too, will become taxable on his return. This type of income is taxed under Schedule D, Case IV or V, and the basis of assessment is the income arising in the previous year (with special treatment in the early and closing years — see below). Because of this previous year basis, the new arrival could find himself with an immediate tax bill on income which arose while he thought he was safely beyond the reach of the Inland Revenue. By a further concession the Revenue do not seek to obtain the full amount of tax chargeable. The assessment for the year of return is restricted to that part of the overseas investment income which corresponds to the fraction of the year during which the taxpayer is actually resident. For example, if an expatriate returns to the United Kingdom on 5 August 1992 he will be resident in the United Kingdom for eight months of tax year 1992/93. If his overseas investment income for 1991/92 was £9,000, the amount assessed for 1992/93 on his return would be:

$$£9,000 \times 8 \div 12 = £6,000$$

If he were to delay his return until 5 March 1993, the assessment then would be on one-twelfth of £9,000, ie £750.

Much as the reduction in these assessments may be welcome, the net result is still a tax liability on income which arose during the non-resident period. In certain circumstances the whole liability can be avoided.

12.1.3   Current year basis

The normal basis of assessment, as stated above, is the income arising in the previous year. But where there is a new source of income, the assessment for the year in which the income first arises is based on the actual income for that year. This is known as the current year basis. One way, therefore, that the returning expatriate can avoid taxation on the previous year basis, is to ensure that when he returns his investments are all recently purchased. This does not mean that the expatriate should make no investments until just before his return. He should, however, sell his securities and repurchase them the next day for a new account or preferably purchase other securities. Similarly, bank deposit accounts should be closed, the money transferred to a current account for a short period and a new deposit account should then be opened.

One point to bear in mind when contemplating the return home and what to do with bank deposits is the period of notice required for withdrawals or closure of the account. Many investors use fixed term deposits for three, six, or 12 months and if the interest rate remains attractive at the end of the term, they simple roll the money over for a subsequent term. Breaking a fixed-term account, if it is permitted at all, will always involve a stiff penalty in interest forfeited. It is essential, therefore, to ensure that all accounts can be terminated before the return date.

The taxation advantage of using this capitalisation or closure procedure can be best illustrated by an example:

Example: Capitalisation of investments

Mr Swan has been abroad for ten years; he opened a deposit account in a Channel Islands bank five years ago and for the last two years the deposit has been standing at £100,000. Interest has been, and for the purpose of illustration, will continue to be, paid at the rate of 10 per cent a year. The interest earned and paid in June and

December has always been withdrawn by Mr Swan and invested elsewhere. Mr Swan's contract ended on 31 December 1991 and he intends to return to the UK on 5 January 1993. If Mr Swan did nothing about his account before coming home he would be assessed for 1992/93 on his interest as follows: interest arising in 1991/92 $\times \frac{1}{4}$ (the portion of the tax year during which he is resident), ie £10,000 $\times \frac{1}{4}$ = £2,500.

If he is taxable only at the basic rate this will mean a bill of £625 payable within 30 days of the issue of the notice of assessment.

If, on the other hand, Mr Swan had closed his account on 31 December 1992 he would have no liability for interest in 1992/93 at all because the first interest payment due from the new source would not be made until June 1993. His first liability would be in 1993/94 and would be calculated on the interest arising in that same year. See Chapter 7 of the *Allied Dunbar Tax Guide*.

The advantage is magnified if, as is often the case, the returned expatriate withdraws a substantial amount of his accrued capital to purchase a house or a business, perhaps. This can be illustrated by considering Mr Swan's actions following his return.

On 1 May 1992 Mr Swan withdraws £50,000 to put towards the purchase of a new house. Assuming in the first instance that he had taken no action over his account before returning, his income tax assessments would be as follows:

1992/93:	on previous year basis (reduced),				£2,500=	tax of	£625
1993/94:	,,	,,	,,	,,	(full),	£10,000=	,,	,,	£2,500
1994/95:	,,	,,	,,	,,	,,	£7,083=	,,	,,	£1,771
1995/96:	,,	,,	,,	,,	,,	£5,000=	,,	,,	£1,250

Thus over the four years he would have paid tax of some £6,146 (assuming that the basic rate of tax continues to be 25 per cent).

If, however, the account had been closed, a totally different picture would emerge. The assessments then would be as follows:

1992/93:	no liability
1993/94:	on current year basis, interest	=£7,083=	tax of £1,771
1994/95:	,,	,,	,,	,,	,,	=£5,000=	,,	,,	£1,250
1995/96:	,,	,,	,,	,,	,,	=£5,000=	,,	,,	£1,250*

In this case the total tax payable over the period is only £4,271, a tax saving of £1,875. (*If a further withdrawal was made in 1995/96, reducing the interest payable in that year, Mr Swan has the option of having that year's income also assessed on the current year basis, reducing his tax charge still further.)

Although this is one of the simplest pieces of tax planning for the returning expatriate, it is often missed. As the example above shows, it can be an expensive omission. But it only works for overseas bank accounts. If the expatriate has held his money on deposit in the United Kingdom he would have had no liability during his period of non-residence but in the year of return this concessionary exemption is lost completely. If nothing is done about a UK account, the full amount of interest paid will be assessed on the previous year basis. There is no apportionment related to the part of the year during which the investor is resident.

If the account is closed before return this will make little, if any, difference. The assessment would then be on the current year basis from the beginning of the tax year to the date of closure and on the same basis from the date of reopening until the following 5 April, ie a full year's interest. The only way around this is to close the UK account in the tax year preceding the tax year of return, transfer the money offshore then use the capitalisation procedure on that offshore account. Because of the hassle involved in this, as well as the need to know the expected return date well in advance, it is better if the expatriate stays clear of UK deposits altogether. The same interest rates, with the same banks, can be obtained outside the United Kingdom.

12.2 Capital gains tax

Turning to the question of CGT, there is now less scope than there used to be for some tax planning tactics. The basic rule is that where a person is not resident and not ordinarily resident throughout the tax year, he will have no liability to UK CGT. By concession, where the tax year is split into a non-resident and resident part in the year of return, no CGT will be charged on gains made during the period of non-residence (ESC D12 (1992)). But to qualify for this treatment, the person must have been non-resident for a continuous period of 36 months. If this condition is not met, then any gains made in the tax year in which the return falls will be taxable whether made before or after the return. For short-term expatriates, therefore, any imminent or potential gains should be realised in the tax year before the year of return. For the longer-term expatriate, gains may be taken without penalty up to the day before returning to the United Kingdom.

The returning expatriate's aim should be to realise his gains before he returns and hold his losses until he rejoins the UK tax system. The converse, of course, will apply if there is a local CGT regime which is more burdensome than that in the United Kingdom. In most cases, however, the investor will not necessarily want to dispose of his holdings. In the case of a married couple where one spouse was resident and the other (the investor) was not resident, the non-resident spouse could transfer the gainful assets to the resident spouse. TCGA 1992, s 58, which normally exempts transfers between husband and wife, does not apply if one of them is non-resident; TCGA 1992, s 288(3) and TA 1988, s 282 *Gubay v Kington* [1984] STC 99. This transfer would be deemed to be carried out at market value and the recipient spouse would have this market value as the acquisition cost. When both spouses were resident in the United Kingdom once more, the asset could be transferred back exempt from tax. Assuming both spouses to be UK-domiciled, there would be no IHT complications. On eventual sale, the base cost would be that market value crystallised on the first transfer, the overall effect being to wipe out gains which arose during the period of non-residence.

Another simple step is the 'bed and breakfast' operation under which investments are sold and repurchased the following day. The repurchase following the previous day's sale (theoretically, and usually in practice too, at the same price or thereabouts) crystallises any underlying gain and gives an enhanced acquisition cost against which to compute the gain on the eventual disposal. It appears from the exchange of correspondence between the Institute of Chartered Accountants and the Revenue, published on 25 September 1985 as TR 588, in para 16, that the *Furniss v Dawson* doctrine would not normally be applied to a properly executed bed and breakfast transaction.

Where the intention is to dispose of certain assets in the near future, perhaps to purchase a house or business, the simplest course might be to sell before return and hold the proceeds on deposit until required. If the assets are showing losses, they should be retained until after return.

So far, this chapter has illustrated ways of reducing the returning expatriate's immediate tax bills. That may be sufficient planning for some expatriates who intend to spend their capital soon after return but for many others it does not go far enough. In particular, where the returning expatriate intends to use his capital to provide an income either to supplement a lower UK salary or to provide a pension in retirement, what is required is longer term planning and the use of a 'tax shelter' and, in this context, good advice is essential.

12.3   Dangers of evasion

Many expatriates believe when they return home that so long as their money is left outside the United Kingdom they will have no UK tax liability on any income arising from that money or any capital gains made. Others believe that they will only have a liability when they remit the income to the United Kingdom. For the British expatriate returning home this is, of course, untrue. Then there are those expatriates who know this to be the case but still take the view that if they leave their money offshore and 'forget' to declare it, the Inland Revenue will never find out. That view, to say the least, is extremely inadvisable. Just one or two points might help to dissuade some expatriates from this course of action.

Assuming that the unlawful evasion goes undetected for a year or two, our evasively-minded individual may decide to spend some of his cash on a new house: the Inland Revenue will receive details of the transaction and any half-awake tax inspector will ask where the balance of the purchase price came from. The claim that it was a legacy from Aunt Freda will not be accepted without sight of the probate documents.

Another myth which should be exploded concerns bank secrecy. More and more countries are co-operating with each other in the transfer of information about taxpayers of mutual interest, and there is often provision for this in double taxation agreements. Even the Swiss banks, those bastions of security where it is a criminal offence to divulge any information about a bank customer, have not proved impregnable to attacks by both the French and American tax authorities. Finally, an incautious word in the golf club may find its way back to the taxman and the subsequent investigation will not be a pleasant experience, quite apart from the substantial costs which will inevitably be incurred.

12.4   Miscellaneous investments

The steps to be taken and the points to be considered with a portfolio of conventional investments have largely been covered, but many expatriates also acquire a range of other investments, whether Persian carpets, Chinese ceramics, precious metals such as bullion, coin or jewellery, and so on. Where these are wanted at home for reasons of aesthetic enjoyment as well as as an investment, the investor should be prepared to pay any necessary duty, including VAT, incurred on importing them. If it is only their investment potential that is of interest, these charges can be avoided by importing them to the Channel Islands and depositing them there. The cost of safe storage and the high cost of insurance, however, must be taken into account.

12.5   Unremittable overseas income

Income from and expenditure on woodlands in the United Kingdom were taken out of the tax system with effect from 15 March 1988, subject to transitional provisions, but woodlands remain a tax efficient investment. They still attract inheritance tax privileges.

Where a person has overseas investment income which cannot be remitted to the United Kingdom or otherwise released from the overseas country, any tax chargeable in the United Kingdom on the income will be held over until such time as the income is released. The unremittability of the income must be by reason of the laws of the overseas country, or executive action of that country's government, or the impossibility of obtaining foreign currency there. In addition the investor must not have realised the income outside that territory for a consideration in sterling or any other freely remittable currency. Where this relief is due it must be claimed before any assessment on the income becomes final. When the income is finally released it will become taxable at that time, and relief will be given for any overseas taxes paid. If the investor dies before the income is released, then any later release will be charged to his personal representatives.

12.6   National Insurance

Some of the benefits available under the British social security system will be accessible to the returning expatriate immediately, regardless of his National Insurance record while overseas, but the major benefits such as unemployment benefit, sickness and invalidity benefit and maternity grants and allowances will only be given where there is an acceptable level of contributions.

Where the returning expatriate has been receiving a National Insurance Retirement Pension at a lower level than that currently prevailing in the United Kingdom he will be entitled to have it uprated to the full rate on his resumption of UK residence.

12.7 Other matters

The returning expatriate must also consider various legal matters. First, he must make sure to give his tenants sufficient notice if he has let his house and wishes to resume living there. It might be considered wise to seek to terminate the tenancy a month or so before the expected date of return to give time for eviction proceedings to be pursued, should the tenants resist moving. The lost rent is unlikely to be as much as the cost of staying in hotels while the law takes its course.

Another point worth watching is the expatriate's will. It may be that he has made a will under his local legal framework while abroad — this is generally no bad thing. The will should be reviewed on return. It may be worth retaining the overseas will, suitably amended, insofar as it relates to property in the overseas country and to have a new will in the United Kingdom. This may assist in releasing overseas assets to the executors in order to pay any IHT required before a grant of probate on the UK will (see also Chapter 8).

Finally, in some countries a tax clearance certificate is required before an exit visa is granted. Where such a certificate is necessary, it is usually essential to apply in good time. There is not a lot of point in turning up at the airport only to be told that you first have to satisfy the local taxman that you have paid all his taxes.

13 Constructing an investment portfolio

Richard Sayer of International Investment Marketing, Allied Dunbar Assurance plc

13.1 Introduction

Depending on your cast of mind or your temperament, you can regard investment as an art, a science, a business or even as a game. But whichever view you adopt, there is no denying the complexity of the subject. For the internationally-orientated investor particularly, the sheer range of investment vehicles and the diversity of criteria for their appraisal are bewildering enough. But in constructing a portfolio there are also many personal factors peculiar to the individual investor that have to be taken into account.

The whole subject is so wide-ranging and important that it merits a book on its own, and for a comprehensive treatment the reader may well like to refer to the *Allied Dunbar Investment and Savings Guide*, which is revised annually to update such key information as stock market performance and changes in tax rules.

This chapter and the following chapters aim to bring out the main points for appraising the major investment media likely to be considered by an expatriate investor. In the following pages we also refer to some of the important tax considerations, but these have been treated in more detail in Chapters 4–11. In choosing an investment, however, the expatriate should bear in mind that the investment itself is generally the primary consideration, and the taxation treatment secondary. In other words, the question of taxation should be decisive only when the benefits of a favourable tax regime tip the balance between investment vehicles that appear to offer returns that are in other respects comparable.

13.2   Establishing objectives

When designing an investment strategy for himself the expatriate should begin with the basic precept that any investment proposal must address his specific financial circumstances. It is not possible to make a considered choice of an investment medium until the objective or purpose of the investment has been established with the utmost clarity. In essence the investor must ask himself three broad questions:

(1)   What do I want my investments to achieve for me?
(2)   In what timescale?
(3)   Within what constraints?

Obviously the more general the question, the more difficult it is to give an accurate, satisfactory and qualified answer. The individual factors that need to be taken into account to arrive at a considered investment strategy are many and varied. The following list is not necessarily exhaustive but it does include the major questions that need to be asked:

(1)   What amount is available for investment, and when?
(2)   What proportion of the total investment portfolio does this represent?
(3)   What other investments are held?
(4)   What part should this investment play in the overall spread and balance of the total portfolio?
(5)   What is the investor's base currency?
(6)   What is the currency of the country to which the investor intends to retire?
(7)   What known liabilities are to be met?
(8)   Is there any expectation of adding to the investment, and when?
(9)   What is the age of the investor and, where relevant, his dependants?
(10) What is the investor's attitude to risk?
(11) What are the access requirements and the likely timescales involved?
(12) What are the personal motivations of the investor?
(13) What is the rate of inflation in the country in which the investor is, and will be, resident?
(14) Is immediate income required from the investment and if so at what level?
(15) Where relevant, what is the required balance between high immediate income and future growth in income?

(16) Is capital appreciation alone the principal present aim?
(17) What are the personal tax liabilities of the investor, both current and expected, and will different rates of tax be applied to income and realised gains?
(18) Are there IHT considerations which may affect the choice of investment?
(19) Are there any other relevant constraints which may limit or influence the choice of investment; for example, exchange controls, protective securities legislation, investment subject to trust, double tax treaties etc?

13.3 Risks and rewards

There is an element of risk in all investment. 'As safe as houses' is a proverbial comment, but in Britain many people bought a flat or a house at the top of the property boom, only to find that they were paying much higher interest on their building society loan than they had planned, while the market price of their property fell or the property proved unsaleable. Similarly, bank deposits are usually instanced as the most risk-free investment you can make, but the purchasing power of the money on deposit can be eroded by inflation which sometimes outstrips interest payments. There have been painful reminders, too, in the last few years that even banks can default. Expatriates are likely to be more exposed than other people to currency risks, and this is such an important consideration that we have devoted two chapters of this Guide to it.

The risks just referred to — of inflation, fraud, or unforeseen and adverse currency movements — can be ruinous, but they are in a sense extraneous or, to use a technical word dear to economists in particular, 'exogenous'. In this section of the Guide we are more concerned with the purely financial risk that investors face. The dictionary defines risk in general as 'the possibility of incurring misfortune or loss', and applied to financial investments this can be further defined as 'the possibility that expected security returns will not materialise and, in particular, that the securities you hold will fall in price'.

Risk so defined is not something to be desired, and most investors are found to be 'risk-averse' whenever their views and feelings are sounded out. All the same, some people imagine that they are more willing than most to take a financial risk. But such people should ask themselves whether they are not really thinking of risking the chance of a gain rather than a loss. The important point is to consider how a particular financial risk is being presented to you. A famous series of experiments has demonstrated that the attractiveness of precisely the same financial risk will normally change depending on whether the risk is presented in terms of an uncertain gain or a possible loss.

For the mathematically minded, financial risk is defined as the variance or standard deviation of returns over time. In other words, a security is risky if its return from year to year is likely to depart appreciably from its average annual return. This means that a security that yields way-out good returns as well as way-out bad is risky in mathematical terms, although in everyday usage only the possibility of the bad or disappointing returns is seen as constituting a risk.

In theory, higher rates of return on an investment incorporate a premium for bearing additional risk. The market with its infinite knowledge (though not its infinite wisdom) is supposed to correlate risk and return in this fashion. Some well-documented studies have shown that it is indeed historically true that investors have received higher rates of return for bearing greater risks. Two American researchers, for example, were able to show that between 1926 and 1983, ordinary shares yielded an annual average rate of return more than three times that of US Treasury Bills, while their risk, calculated in terms of standard deviations, was nearly seven times as great. (In one year in three, shares showed a negative return, which was true of Treasury Bills in only one year out of the 58 surveyed.)

An important practical consequence of this relationship between risk and reward is that you should always look very hard indeed at any investment which claims to yield a well-above-average return. For one reason or another, such an investment or investment proposal is absolutely bound to be even more-than-well-above-average risky. After all, the American research just quoted showed that investors had to take on seven times as much volatility to get three times as much return, and as this research covered the entire stock market, it took care only of average or market risk, and not the particular risk inevitably associated with an individual stock or investment scheme.

A particular word that should put all investors on their guard is 'guaranteed'. This word has no legal force unless it really does mean a bankable guarantee — implying some form of collateral backing the claimed return. If an intermediary claims to guarantee a specific return, ask him who or what guarantees it, and whether his guarantee has any legal status.

The best way of reducing financial risk is through diversification. Here the proverbial wisdom about not putting all your eggs in one basket really does apply (and its truth has in fact been demonstrated by rigorous mathematical argument). In spite of this, it is surprising how many investors pay little heed to this truth. But in diversifying or spreading your investments, you should bear in mind that there is a general market (sometimes called 'systematic') risk besides the risk inherent in the shares of a particular company ('unsystematic risk'). In other words, it's possible to see your widely-spread equity investments all go down together (as they may all rise together in a bull market).

13.3.1 Some rules of thumb

Below is a list of points to consider:

(1) The degree of future risk in any investment is always a matter of judgment. Mathematical measures of performance, volatility or risk hold water only when applied to the past.
(2) The longer you are prepared to tie your money up, the greater the return you are entitled to expect.
(3) The riskier an investment appears to be, the greater the return you should expect.
(4) In general, the various investment media can be put on a scale of financial risk as follows:
    (a) Commodities: extremely risky.
    (b) Equities (shares in public companies): here the risk varies greatly from company to company, but there is also the general market risk referred to above.
    (c) Corporate bonds: less risky than equity, because the capital itself is not normally at risk.
    (d) Collective investments (unit trusts, mutual funds, investment trusts): less risky still, because the investment is spread among many different shares, bonds, or other media.
    (e) Life assurance: the only risk arises if you are unable to keep paying the premiums, as there may be a heavy penalty for early cancellation.
    (f) Bank and building society deposits: normally no risk at all.
    (g) Government stocks: such as gilts — the fixed-interest

stocks issued or guaranteed by the British government. Financially the safest investment of all (but depending on the issuing government and on the investor's base currency, still subject to the risk of erosion by inflation and to currency risk).

13.3.2   Investor protection

After some notorious cases of fraud and malpractice (some of them on a vast scale) in recent years, jurisdictions all over the world are reviewing and tightening their authorisation and regulation of financial intermediaries of all kinds.

In the United Kingdom, the Securities and Investment Board (SIB) acts as an umbrella organisation for a number of Self-Regulatory Organisations (SROs) set up to provide proper regulation of the investment business carried on in different financial sectors. The SIB is a private limited company whose costs of operation are met by the UK financial services sector (embracing the stock market, unit trusts, life assurance, pension fund management and private portfolio management), but it reports directly to ministers of the Crown. Its board members are appointed jointly by the Economic Secretary at the Treasury and by the Governor of the Bank of England. The SIB's powers derive from the Financial Services Act 1986 (see **1.2.2**), and this Act also makes provision for recognised professional bodies such as the three Institutes of Chartered Accountants and the Law Society to authorise their members to carry on investment business (mainly in the form of advice) as part of their professional services to their clients.

Expatriates investing in the United Kingdom, or taking advice from or in some way availing themselves of the services of a UK intermediary should make sure that the company or intermediary concerned is a member of an SRO or recognised professional body. A list of relevant addresses is given in Appendix III.

The self-regulatory system seems to be peculiar to the United Kingdom, most other jurisdictions regulating the financial services sector directly from the Central Bank or equivalent body, or a government department or agency, or from a combination of these two entities. If you are planning to invest offshore, you should find out which is the local authority responsible for authorisation and regulation, and then make sure that the particular investment or company you are contemplating is properly subject to this authority. Further details about particular offshore centres are also given in Appendix III.

13.4 Constructing a portfolio

Choosing the individual components of an investment portfolio can be confusing. Performance statistics often serve to mislead rather than inform. There is a disturbing tendency these days, among some sectors of the financial press, to measure investment performance over unrealistically short timescales. Apart from causing confusion when attempting to compare the performance of different shares, sectors or investment funds, it makes comparisons between different investment media meaningless. Perhaps the most important difference between the mainstream investment areas is the time-frame within which they can be expected to provide effective performance. The prudent investor will use published investment statistics with caution, taking care to obtain sufficient information to indicate clearly the track record of his chosen investment.

So armed with all this information, what kind of investment does the expatriate need to satisfy his aims? Where should he start looking?

Leaving aside the esoteric sorts of 'investment' opportunities — emeralds, rare stamps, coffee futures and the like — most private investors will find their needs catered for by the mainstream investment areas — bank deposits, government bonds and equities. These three areas account for well over 90 per cent of privately invested monies. Before we go on to examine specific investment vehicles, we will look at the main characteristics of these media.

Monies placed on deposit have a secure capital value in money terms, but the income produced will vary depending on the prevailing interest rate. This means, contrary to popular belief, that the overall return from a deposit is far from guaranteed. If we go further and consider the overall return in real-value terms (as opposed to the meaningless 'money' return), it is clear that in an inflationary climate the longer the investment is held the more vulnerable it becomes.

An investment in government bonds is almost the reverse of this situation in that the income is generally guaranteed (in money terms) but now the capital value will fluctuate, depending again on the prevailing interest rate climate. The bond will usually have a guaranteed capital value at redemption, of course, but once again only in money terms, not in real value.

It will be seen that in the case of the two main investment areas where genuine guarantees are common, the main effect of the guarantee is to provide a secure and dependable return in the short term, but to restrict the overall return over the longer term. If one is looking for realistic growth rates over longer timescales, experience has shown that they have only been achieved by investments in real assets such as shares, which produce both income and a capital return.

There can be no guarantees or predictions but in a capitalist society, which is expected to remain so, security will more likely be achieved in the long term by investing in a well balanced carefully managed portfolio of equities — providing the investor's timescales are long enough to iron out the fluctuations caused by the ebbs and flows in world market conditions and the changes in market sentiment generated by political climates. Historically, five years upwards has been the right sort of timescale to consider equity investment to have sufficient security. If equity investment is contemplated over shorter periods than this, it stands the risk of being speculation rather than an investment.

Most investment advisers would, for the majority of their clients, recommend a balance between the highly liquid, short-term, high income bank/money market deposit, and the longer term equity-linked investment, offering capital appreciation, with characteristic fluctuations in value and a lower but secure percentage income yield. The actual income will rise as the capital value appreciates and this element of the portfolio is therefore the key to providing the growth in income that is necessary to offset the erosive effects of inflation. The middle ground will be held by government bonds (such as gilt-edged stock or Eurobonds).

Quite how the proportion between deposits, bonds and equity-linked investment will be determined, depends on the answers to the list of questions at **13.3.1**, and hence the particular needs of the individual investor. As a rule of thumb (and a potentially hazardous one, since any such rule must make assumptions about average needs) a classically constructed portfolio might have anywhere between £2,000 and £20,000 on deposit. Of the balance, one quarter to one third might be in bonds, with the rest in equity-linked investments (frequently mutual funds such as unit trusts or offshore funds).

To summarise:

(1) There must be a spread of investment sufficient to contain the volatility and depreciation risks that are incurred with an overly weighted exposure to one investment medium, one market sector, one country or one currency.
(2) Within individual stockmarket holdings there should be a balanced mix of investment sectors eg manufacturing, engineering, property, finance, leisure etc.
(3) The resulting portfolio must be under active daily management to ensure that the results obtained continue to meet the investor's needs.

Clearly, this is an ideal situation which the average investor may find difficult or impossible to achieve by direct investment. He may not have the expertise to guide his choice or the time to manage a balanced portfolio actively. Even where the time and expertise are to hand, the required spread may be impossible to achieve in all but the largest private portfolios without striking 'minimum bargains' where the dealing costs are disproportionately high.

For many investors, the answer is to construct their portfolio from large building blocks such as the wide range of collective investment media that are available. The main areas from which the choice may be made are described in the following chapters.

14 Bank and building society deposits

14.1 Banking services for expatriates

Whether an individual's financial affairs are very simple or extremely complex, successful financial planning begins with establishing proper and effective banking arrangements. Apart from providing a home for money in its own right, a bank provides the mechanisms which link and give access to whatever other financial arrangements need to be made.

Specific individual requirements will depend on personal circumstances, but most expatriates are likely to need some or all of the following services from their bank:

(1) Sterling current account: expatriates tend to keep higher balances than their onshore counterparts so this should, preferably, be interest bearing;
(2) sterling deposit account: as mentioned earlier this forms an important part in constructing a secure investment portfolio;
(3) currency deposit account: many expatriates are paid in foreign currency and, according to their domestic arrangements, may well have this currency as their base currency giving rise to a need for appropriate deposit facilities;
(4) currency conversion facilities;
(5) loan facilites: expatriates will often have the need for both short and longer-term borrowing, perhaps in the latter instance to buy a home in the United Kingdom;
(6) standing orders;
(7) direct debit facilities;
(8) international money transfers;
(9) eurocheque facilities;
(10) credit card payment facilities;
(11) international money orders and drafts.

Most banks, whether in the United Kingdom or offshore, can provide these services. But apart from considerations of tax (discussed immediately below), there are other good reasons for the expatriate to conduct as much of his banking business as possible offshore. In the first place, he has many particular requirements and problems that UK residents do not have, and these are more likely to be understood and catered for by an offshore bank or branch that specialises in the banking needs of expatriates. Indeed, we know of cases where expatriates have been incorrectly or misleadingly advised by local branch managers in the United Kingdom who did not have specialised knowledge or experience of expatriate personal finance.

There are two further important advantages to the expatriate if his bank or branch operates from either the Channel Islands or the Isle of Man:

(1) These offshore centres are outside the UK tax jurisdiction, but have access to the UK banking network. This means that the full facilities of a UK clearing bank, such as cheque books and credit and other plastic cards for use in the United Kingdom, can be made available.

(2) Jersey, Guernsey, and the Isle of Man have comprehensive financial services legislation enacted which assures the investor of substantially the same safeguards and protection as if he had made his financial arrangements with an institution in the United Kingdom. The Isle of Man, moreover, is the first offshore centre to operate a deposit protection scheme, which covers 75 per cent of the first £20,000 of a deposit, whether in sterling or in a foreign currency.

14.2 Bank and building society deposits

At the beginning of Chapter 13, we said that taxation was generally a secondary consideration to the actual nature of a particular investment medium. But in the matter of bank or building society deposits taxation can often be the first question you should consider. This is because interest arising on an account or deposit in a bank or building society in the United Kingdom is a UK source of income for a non-UK resident. In certain circumstances, under an extra-statutory concession, this interest is not taxable for non-residents, but the rules are complex, especially as they apply to the non-resident's year of departure from and year of return to the United Kingdom. These rules are explained in full detail in Chapter 4.

There is the further point that for an investor not domiciled in the United Kingdom, a deposit in the United Kingdom is treated as a UK sited asset for purposes of IHT, unless the deposit is in a currency other than sterling. This point is explained in greater detail in Chapter 7.

Many, though not all, of these UK tax problems can be avoided by a non-resident if he puts his bank deposits offshore. This is an area in which banks and building societies compete, and there is a very wide range of savings or deposit accounts on offer. But broadly speaking, the accounts fall into three main categories:

(1) deposit or savings accounts with variable interest rates (the rates changing from time to time in line with base rates or money market rates);
(2) high interest cheque accounts (often money market accounts);
(3) fixed-term deposits, where interest rates are usually based on prevailing money market rates for the duration of the term, and the interest is paid on maturity.

The differences between the terms offered by rival institutions relate to such matters as the minimum deposit required and the minimum notice of withdrawal (which also tend to affect the rate of interest offered), the variation between the rates of interest paid on deposits of different amounts, and the periodicity of crediting the account with interest. The choice between the three categories mentioned will depend not only on the particular conditions attached, but, especially if you opt for a fixed-term deposit, on your own view of the likely future course of interest rates. Surveys of the terms and conditions offered by offshore institutions are published from time to time in the *Financial Times* magazine for British expatriates, *Resident Abroad*.

As far as deposits are concerned, there is no difference in principle between an offshore bank or branch of a bank and an offshore branch of a UK building society. In recent years, moreover, the major UK building societies have extended their range of services to include many that previously only banks supplied, such as cheque books and plastic cards, standing order/direct debit facilities, and so on. But they are unlikely to provide the full range of services required by the expatriate investor.

Finally, one general caveat applies to deposits, whether in a bank or a building society: this part of an investor's portfolio should not be allowed to grow out of proportion to the rest of the portfolio, because there is no possibility of growth of the original capital in the case of a deposit (as distinct from any accruals of interest that may be allowed to accumulate).

15   Fixed-interest securities

15.1   British government stocks

British government stocks (also known as British funds, gilts, or
gilt-edged securities) are the instrument used by the government
and certain nationalised industries to raise capital. The stocks are
guaranteed by the government and consequently are totally secure.
Investors can be sure that the stated rate of interest will be paid and
the nominal principal returned, in accordance with the provisions
of the loan.

Gilt-edged securities normally have a fixed rate of interest, known
as the 'coupon', which is expressed as a percentage of the nominal
value; so, for example, the holder of £100 nominal of Treasury
Loan 8¾ per cent 1997 will receive £8.75 a year until that date
(normally subject to deduction of income tax at the basic rate — but
see below) regardless of the price at which he purchased the stock
or its market value from time to time. In addition to paying interest
during the life of the stock, the government also has a requirement
to repay the loan at the nominal or par value of £100, on the date
stated — this is known as the redemption date.

The market value at any given time will depend upon the coupon,
the amount of time to run to redemption and prevailing interest
rate conditions. The closer a stock is to redemption the nearer the
market price will be to the nominal value. Stocks are usually
classified according to the length of time to run to redemption, as
follows:

(1)   'shorts': five years or less to redemption;
(2)   'mediums': between five and 15 years to redemption;
(3)   'longs': over 15 years to redemption.

In addition there are also undated or irredeemable stocks with no
final date specified for redemption.

For the mediums and longs, at least, the key factor in determining their capital value from time to time is the prevailing structure of interest rates compared with the coupon on the stock. If the prevailing interest rate falls, the value of the stock will rise. This is because a larger investment is required at the new rate to give an equivalent yield. If the prevailing interest rate falls below the stock's coupon, then the value of the stock will rise above its par value and the stock can be sold for a tax-free capital gain (British government stocks being exempt from CGT, no matter how long they are held, and irrespective of the fiscal residence status of the holder). Conversely, if interest rates rise, then the capital value of the stock will fall, and if interest rates rise above the coupon, the stock's price will fall below par, and if sold then would generate a capital loss.

The expatriate buying gilts directly (as distinct from via a collective investment vehicle) should generally choose from the range of so-called 'exempt' or 'approved' stocks, where the income can be paid gross (ie without the normal deduction of basic rate income tax at source) to an individual not ordinarily resident in the United Kingdom. Details of the stocks currently exempt and advice on the procedure needed to get the interest paid gross are given in Chapter 4 at **4.4**.

Because the investment is guaranteed by the government and the coupon and redemption value are both fixed, gilt-edged securities are ideal for the investor who places a high premium on security. The wide range of stocks on the market, however, and the complex calculations sometimes needed to compare redemption yields make it advisable to have some expert advice before investing even in these safe securities, and for this reason many investors prefer a collective medium to direct investment.

15.2 Bulldog bonds

'Bulldog bonds' is an informal term used to designate sterling-denominated fixed-interest bonds issued by foreign governments and international agencies in the British domestic market. The structure of such bonds is fundamentally similar to that of the gilts issued by the British government, but they are usually priced to yield ½–1 per cent more than the nearest equivalent gilt. Depending on the method of sale, bulldog bonds are quoted either in the debenture market or in the gilt-edged market. Several of the issues have features that are unavailable on gilt-edged stocks, such as investors' options for repayment at par after a certain number of years. The interest is paid gross on some issues.

15.3   Eurobonds

Eurobonds developed from the market in Eurodollars, which originated in the 1950s as claims for US dollars in the hands of banks and their clients outside the United States who did not want to transfer their money to the United States. The market gradually extended to other major currencies held by persons not living in the country of the currency concerned.

Eurobonds are now issued in most of the world's major currencies, with the Japanese yen and the deutschemark sectors the most active. The bonds are issued by consortia of banks (the primary market) on behalf of the borrowers (mostly large corporations or governments and their agencies), and the banks may then sell them to investors (the secondary market), most of whom are institutions.

Some private individuals find Eurobonds attractive, partly because they are usually issued in bearer form, which means there is no register of holders, and ownership of them can be transferred as easily as ownership of a bank note; and partly because the interest on a Eurobond is always paid (on presentation of the coupon) without any deduction of tax.

There are three main types of Eurobond:

(1)   straights: which carry a fixed-interest coupon and a fixed maturity date;
(2)   floating rate notes (FRNs): which have an interest rate tied to an agreed (but fluctuating) international rate, usually the London interbank offered rate (LIBOR);
(3)   convertibles: which are convertible to ordinary shares on the terms stated.

The *Financial Times* gives extensive coverage to this market on its International Capital Markets and Companies page. Its table of Eurobond prices is headed 'FT/ISMA International Bond Service'.

You can buy Eurobonds either through your stockbroker or your bank, but there will not be much enthusiasm on your intermediary's part unless you are investing at least £25,000 in this medium.

Another point to consider is that you cannot always sell your Eurobonds when you want to, owing to illiquidity in the market resulting from the attitude of the main players in the market to such factors as currency fluctuations or even political uncertainty. On the positive side, however, for the private investor wishing to have a share of the action in Eurobonds, there are a number of offshore funds (see Chapter 17) specialising in collective Eurobond investment.

15.4 Corporate bonds

The relatively high rate of inflation in the United Kingdom throughout most of the post-war period has caused most private individuals to prefer company shares to bonds, whereas the opposite has been true in countries with historically low rates of inflation, such as Germany and Switzerland. As this book goes to press, this historical comparison of inflation rates looks like being reversed, but perhaps only temporarily, in favour of the United Kingdom. In spite of this, however, it is unlikely that large numbers of individual British investors will switch their preference to the corporate bond market.

Companies issue two types of fixed-interest vehicles: debentures, which are backed by specific assets of the issuer; and loan stocks, some of which are secured while others are not. Corporate bonds offer a higher yield than gilts, because even a blue-chip company is considered riskier than the British government, but against this advantage it is not always as easy to sell corporate bonds back to the market as it is to dispose of gilts. The most convenient way to deal in corporate bonds is through a stockbroker, who will also be able to explain the pros and cons of certain special types of bond such as convertibles and deep discount bonds.

16   Direct investment in equities

16.1   Useful publications

The subject of direct investment in ordinary shares of quoted companies calls not so much for a separate chapter, but for an entire book, if not an encyclopaedia. And not surprisingly, several publishers have already answered that call. The *Investors Chronicle*, the FT's weekly magazine for stock market enthusiasts, has issued a so-called Beginner's Guide to the stock market as such, and another to investment in general, which are both very useful and which both go well beyond the mere beginnings of the subject.

The *Allied Dunbar Investment and Savings Guide*, already referred to in Chapter 13, contains a chapter on listed investments which not only reviews the highlights of the previous year's activity on the UK stock market, with brief references to other important markets round the world, but bravely previews some of the major probable trends in the year ahead. In the same chapter you will also find a detailed explanation of the actual mechanics of dealing on The Stock Exchange.

For investors interested in the strategy and tactics of stock market investment, it is difficult to think of a better book than Burton G Malkiel's modern classic *A Random Walk down Wall Street*, published also in London by W W Norton & Company. Although written primarily for US readers, this book contains a great deal of material of both theoretical and practical interest to investors in equities, wherever they may be. Mr Malkiel tends to take a sceptical view of technical systems and theories, and he stresses the overriding importance of the time element in stock market investment. Indeed, he defines true investment, as distinct from speculation, as 'a method of purchasing assets in order to gain profit in the form of reasonably predictable income and/or (capital) appreciation over the long term'.

16.2   Individual investors: risks and potential advantages

In spite of the domination of nearly all the stock markets in the world, and certainly the major ones, by professional investors managing institutional funds, all the authors just mentioned express the view that there is still scope for the private individual investor. The editor's postbag at *Resident Abroad* shows, too, that a great many expatriates are still interested in DIY equity investment, even though they may at the same time hold units in one or other type of investment fund. The well-known investment consultant Peter Doye has a regular column in the magazine intended for such expatriate investors.

It is true that the comparatively small individual investor has high costs in the way of brokerage charges and perhaps fees for ancillary services such as advice, and that the spread between the buying and selling prices of ordinary shares is such that their market price has to rise by 6 or 7 per cent (even more in the case of some of the smaller companies) before the investor can see a profit. But similar considerations apply to investment funds, which also charge annual management fees.

Some individual investors persist down the direct route into equities for the personal satisfaction or even excitement that cannot be experienced when your only stake is in a large pool of assets being managed not only on your behalf but on behalf of perhaps hundreds of other investors. A more important consideration with some individual investors, however, is this: a collective investment by definition spreads the risk, and thereby to some extent limits the possible reward, even if at the same time it limits the possible loss. Spread as a collective investment is across a number of securities, its performance will tend to be related more closely to the market or sector average than will the performance of a particular share. In other words, it is possible if you pick the shares of the right companies to make spectacular profits (and equally astonishing losses if you pick the wrong shares), which is hardly the case even with the highest performing collective funds.

Bernard Gray, in the *Beginners' Guide to Investment*, the second of the *Investors Chronicle* books referred to above, suggests other ways in which the private investor may have the edge over the professional: 'he does not have to produce quarterly figures showing his relative performance, as fund managers do. Nor does he have to remain in the market when he would sooner be out. He can buy shares because he genuinely likes their investment prospects, not because he fears being left behind by the market. And he can buy into all but the smallest companies without moving the market price to his disadvantage'. In spite of the professional's easy access to far more information about companies and markets than is normally available to the private individual, the private individual is sometimes able, by a mixture of common sense, lateral thinking, and a modicum of luck, to pick winners that the professionals miss. One expatriate investor of our acquaintance made a considerable fortune in this way. For example, when one national motorway building programme was getting under way he reasoned, ahead of the professionals, that road sign manufacturers would have a bonanza, and he was able to buy a fair stake in such a company before his and eventually other investors' shrewdness caused it to become a favourite. But here we must put in a word of warning. Playing the stock market in this way can easily be addictive, and grow from something akin to a hobby to a full-time occupation, if not an obsession.

There are between 40 and 50 national stock markets throughout the world, and new ones are established every year, but the expatriate will probably have to be very well established in his host country before he deals on the local exchange. He is much more likely to deal through a London stockbroker or bank, through whom he will be able to buy most major stocks in the world. For more adventurous trading than this he will usually be better advised to consider a unit trust or offshore fund specialising in a particular national market, rather than dealing directly.

17 Collective investment vehicles

Pauline Skypala, former Deputy Editor, Resident Abroad

17.1 Introduction

Direct investment in the share, fixed-interest and currency markets is often not an option for expatriates, who do not always have the time or the information to run their own investment portfolios, even if they have the expertise and the inclination. And there are few investment managers who are prepared to undertake direct investment on behalf of anyone with less than around £250,000 to invest.

Instead, they advocate the use of collective investment vehicles such as investment trusts, unit trusts and offshore funds, all of which work on the same basic principle: a pooling of resources which enables small investors to participate in a professionally managed portfolio of shares, benefiting from a spread of risk that they could not achieve on their own. However, it is important to realise that you can still lose money – pooled funds do not protect you from a falling stock market.

The main differences between the various types of collective investment vehicle are related to structure, location and taxation. Offshore funds are generally recommended as the most appropriate vehicles for the expatriate investor, but there are also arguments in favour of using UK-based funds in some circumstances. But before reviewing the pros and cons of offshore and onshore funds, it is useful to examine their workings.

17.2   UK investment and unit trusts

17.2.1   UK investment trusts

These were the first pooled funds to be established, although they are probably the least familiar to the investing public. They are public companies, listed on The Stock Exchange, which invest in the shares of other companies in the United Kingdom and overseas. They are described as 'closed end', which means that there is a fixed number of shares in existence and the fund does not expand or contract.

Investment trusts offer a wide range of investment opportunities: there are general trusts with an international portfolio; specific geographic trusts covering the United Kingdom, North America, Japan, Europe, etc; trusts investing in specific industrial sectors, such as smaller companies, financial and property; trusts that invest for capital growth, and trusts that aim for a high income; plus specialist vehicles such as venture capital and split capital trusts.

You can buy shares in an investment trust through a stockbroker, bank, building society or other share dealing service. Because of the minimum commission often charged on stock market dealings, however, this method is mainly suitable for large share purchases. Smaller investors can use an investment trust savings and investment scheme. These allow the occasional investment of lump sums of just £250 plus, or a regular monthly investment of as little as £25. Charges vary, but are in most cases low, and in some cases nil. Most schemes also offer special selling arrangements which are often cheaper than the normal rate of broker's commission.

Annual management charges on investment trusts are also relatively low compared with those on other pooled investment schemes, averaging 0.5 per cent of assets under management.

The prices of investment trust shares are set by the stock market and are governed by the same laws of supply and demand which affect all share prices. Note that the share price may be at a premium or a discount to the net asset value (NAV) per share, which expresses the actual value of a trust's assets after the deduction of the value of its preference shares and all its liabilities.

If the share price is at a discount to the net asset value you are buying assets at a lower cost than you would pay if you bought them directly on the stock market; if it is at a premium, you are paying more. Most investment trust shares trade at a discount.

17.2.2   UK unit trusts

These differ from investment trusts in being structured as trust funds rather than investment companies, in which you buy units rather than shares. They are 'open-ended', which means the managers can create or redeem units to match demand, and must increase or reduce their shareholdings depending on whether money is coming in or going out of the fund. Unit trusts are not usually quoted on the stock market.

You can buy units directly from the management companies, or through an independent financial adviser. Prices are fixed by the managers in accordance with rules specified by the Securities and Investment Board (SIB) and reflect the value of the assets held. Two prices are given, an *offer price* which includes the 'initial charge' you pay to buy units, which is usually between 5 and 6 per cent; and the lower *bid price* for selling. Annual management charges average 1.25 per cent. You can invest a lump sum or use a savings plan to invest smaller amounts on a regular basis. There is usually no extra charge involved in these plans.

Like investment trusts, unit trusts give you access to stock markets around the world and to specialist investment sectors, including fixed-interest and money market instruments.

Investments in unit trusts and investment trusts receive the same tax treatment. The funds themselves do not pay CGT on any profits they make, but UK resident investors may be liable for the tax on any gains realised when they sell if they are in excess of the annual allowance. Income distributions are paid effectively net of basic rate tax, ie with a tax credit. Non-taxpayers may reclaim the amount credited.

17.3   Offshore funds

A fund is described as 'offshore' if it is incorporated in a low tax financial centre such as the Isle of Man, the Channel Islands, or Luxembourg, and intended for use by non-residents of that jurisdiction. Such funds generally pay little or nothing in the way of local taxes, although they may receive dividends or interest net of withholding tax, depending on where and in which instruments they invest. They are usually structured as open-ended investment companies or unit trusts, able to issue and redeem their own shares or units. Offshore fund prices reflect the value of the underlying assets, but some funds work on a dual pricing system, quoting both an offer and a bid price, while others work on a single pricing system.

The charging structure of offshore funds is similar to that of UK unit trusts, with an initial charge of nil to 5 or 6 per cent, depending on the type of underlying investment, and an annual charge of 0.5 to 2 per cent, again varying with the type and location of a fund's holdings.

Offshore funds offer a wide choice of investment opportunities and management groups. They provide an investment route into virtually every stock market in the world, most freely exchangeable currencies, Eurobonds, government bonds, commodities, financial derivatives (futures, options and warrants), and even property. If you know which areas you want to invest in you can choose specific funds, or you can opt for an international fund where the investment decisions about which markets to go into are made by the managers.

Many offshore funds are set up as umbrella funds, which simply means that instead of running separate funds the managers run one inclusive fund split into a number of sub-funds. This offers advantages for the managers, mainly in the shape of more cost-efficient administration, and generally makes it easier and cheaper for investors to switch between different investment areas.

Some offshore funds distribute the income they earn on their investments, while others accumulate it within the fund. The latter type are often more convenient for expatriate investors, but may not be suitable if you are intending to return to the United Kingdom in the near future. This is because the tax treatment of offshore funds in the United Kingdom depends on whether the fund has distributor status or not. An investment in a fund with distributor status is taxed in the same way as a UK unit trust. But if you hold a fund without distributor status, you are liable for income tax on both the income from the fund and any capital gain you make on disposal.

Thus, investments in a non-distributor fund need to be sold during a period of non-residence, and unless you can be sure that you will be overseas for some years or that you will have the opportunity to sell your holding in a subsequent period of non-residence, it is sensible to opt for a distributor fund. Most such funds have a reinvestment facility for investors who do not want to receive dividends.

Do not assume that a fund which distributes its income automatically has distributor status. The majority do, but to be granted the status, they have to satisfy certain rules, the most important of which is that they distribute at least 85 per cent of the income earned on their investments.

The major centres for offshore funds are the Channel Islands, Luxembourg, Hong Kong, the Isle of Man, and to a growing extent, Ireland. Also notable are Bermuda and the Cayman Islands, and Gibraltar, too, is competing for offshore fund business. You will find that some funds are incorporated in one jurisdiction but administered and managed from another, usually for tax reasons. For example, a fund based in Bermuda may be run from Jersey, with investment advice coming from London. This is of little concern to investors as far as investment performance or taxation are concerned, but could affect whether or not they are covered by a compensation scheme.

Regulation in these centres is relatively good, having been tightened considerably in recent years in response to changes in the marketplace, such as the advent of the single European market for financial services, the introduction of the Financial Services Act in the United Kingdom, and various scandals — notably the collapse of the Savings & Investment Bank in the Isle of Man and the Barlow Clowes affair.

The first two factors in particular have occasioned the introduction of different categories of funds, and although this has limited practical significance for the investor, the terminology can be confusing. One of the main distinctions to be aware of is that between so-called Ucits funds and other offshore funds. Ucits is shorthand for Undertaking for Collective Investment in Transferable Securities, and denotes an open-ended fund that has complied with certain requirements, laid down in a European Community Directive, which allow it to be marketed freely in all European Community countries, subject to local marketing regulations.

Ucits funds have to be based in an EC member country, and most of the funds that have been set up specifically to take advantage of the single European market for financial services are based in Luxembourg, although Dublin is also becoming an important centre. However, it makes little difference to the investor whether or not a fund is a Ucits; the significance of a fund's status in this respect is mainly of interest to fund managers and financial advisers.

Other categories of funds you may come across also relate mainly to where the funds can be marketed. Jersey, Guernsey and the Isle of Man, for example, have two or three classifications which funds can slot into, depending on whether or not the managers want to market them in the United Kingdom. There are no Ucits funds in these three centres, as they are all outside the EC for most purposes (with the exception of the free movement of industrial and agricultural goods). But to enable fund managers to promote their products to UK investors, the Channel Islands and the Isle of Man (and Bermuda) applied to become designated territories under the UK Financial Services Act. This entailed providing investor protection at least equivalent to the cover given to investors in UK unit trusts, and to comply with this all the islands set up compensation schemes.

In Jersey and the Isle of Man, the compensation scheme provides for a maximum sum of £48,000, made up of 100 per cent of the first £30,000 and 90 per cent of the next £20,000, in line with the benefits provided under the UK scheme. The Guernsey scheme offers a maximum payout of £60,000, comprising 90 per cent of the first £50,000 and 30 per cent of the next £50,000. All recognised or authorised class funds in the islands are covered by the schemes. But this by no means includes all the funds based in the islands, so it is wise to check if you want to know for certain whether you are covered by a compensation scheme.

17.3.1   Advantages of offshore funds

The main attractions of offshore funds are their freedom from tax, the confidentiality factor, and the wide range of investments they offer, including currency funds which are not available at all onshore.

Where offshore funds really score on the tax front is on the income side, as they are able to pay the investor an income from investments in instruments such as Eurobonds, deposits, and exempt gilts without the deduction of any tax. In contrast, investors in UK gilt, fixed-interest and money market funds receive income payments net of 25 per cent tax. As a result, fixed-interest and money market funds comprise a significant proportion of the offshore funds available and are widely used by expatriates.

When it come to investment for capital growth, however, there is little difference between offshore funds and UK unit or investment trusts in terms of tax: they all accumulate investment profits free of CGT. Whether the income and capital gains earned on offshore fund investments remain tax-free in the hands of the investor obviously depends on where he is resident when he receives them.

If tax is not the deciding factor in using offshore funds, the scales may be tipped in their favour by other considerations, in particular the currency factor, which plays an important role in the financial affairs of expatriate investors. All UK pooled funds are denominated in sterling regardless of where they invest, whereas offshore funds are frequently denominated in the currency of their main investment area. Thus, North American funds are quoted in dollars, Far East funds in Hong Kong dollars or Japanese yen, and European funds in deutschemarks or Swiss francs.

In addition to providing currency exposure in this way, offshore funds also offer a means of investing in foreign currency deposits and bonds. These funds are available either on a managed basis, where the managers make the investment decisions about which currencies to hold, or on an individual currency basis where the individual decides on the currency mix. The advantage such funds offer over using bank deposits to hold foreign currency is that they give smaller investors access to money market rates of interest.

17.3.2 Disadvantages of offshore funds

There are few real disadvantages to using offshore funds, although some commentators maintain that if you are planning to return to the United Kingdom, it makes life simpler if you stick to UK funds. There is no question then of having to sell your investment at an inopportune moment to avoid unwelcome tax consequences on your return to the United Kingdom, as you might have to if you have any non-distributor funds in your portfolio. Many expatriates prefer to keep their investments outside the United Kingdom while they are non-resident, however, and the simplest way to avoid any tax complications with offshore funds is to make sure you invest only in funds with distributor status.

Another worry with offshore funds is regulation. A widely held view is that offshore fund groups are not as tightly regulated as UK fund groups. There is some substance in this, but as noted above, Ucits, recognised and authorised funds are all allowed to be sold to UK residents, and should therefore be subject to the same degree of regulation by the appropriate authorities. If you are concerned about this aspect of using offshore funds, it is as well to restrict your choice to funds of this type. The other safeguard is to use only funds run by big international groups or by fund managers that are well-known in the United Kingdom.

It is sometimes suggested that offshore funds tend to perform less well than UK funds, owing to a combination of higher charges and lower quality investment management. But while it is the case that offshore funds do carry slightly higher charges on average than unit trusts, this is unlikely to have a significant effect on performance. Moreover, the charge that offshore funds do not receive the same attention as a group's UK funds is difficult to prove, and one that many groups keen to earn a good reputation for investment performance on an international stage would doubtless contend.

There is no consistent statistical evidence to support the contention that UK funds are the better performers, and comparisons are in any case questionable because of the currency factor. Much depends on which currency you use to measure performance: a fund denominated in US dollars investing in the United States may look lacklustre compared with a similar vehicle valued in sterling if the pound has fallen against the dollar over the investment period.

17.3.3 How to invest in offshore funds

You can invest in an offshore fund either by contacting the managers directly or via your financial adviser. Many investment managers will run a portfolio of offshore funds for you, or you can put together your own. Some fund managers will accept only lump sum investments, but quite a few also offer a non-contractual regular savings scheme.

You can check the prices of offshore funds in the *Financial Times*, which carries listings every day. The paper lists funds by area and according to whether they are SIB recognised, regulated or other. SIB recognised funds are those which are allowed to be marketed to the general public in the United Kingdom, such as Ucits funds. Regulated funds are those which are not SIB recognised but are regulated by the authorities of the jurisdiction in which they are based. Funds categorised as 'other' are mostly based in jurisdictions such as Hong Kong, the Cayman Islands, the Bahamas, etc, which are neither EC member states nor designated territories under the Financial Services Act. Note that addresses are given only for the managers of SIB recognised funds.

Performance figures for offshore funds are carried in specialist magazines such as *Resident Abroad*, the *International* and *Investment International*. When choosing an offshore fund or fund group, look for consistent performers rather than chart toppers. Ideally, you should select funds run by management groups that can produce above-average performance across the whole range of their funds. This is particularly important if you opt to use an umbrella fund, as you are then relying solely on the investment expertise of one group, and there are only a few that are equally good in all investment sectors.

18   Life assurance

Richard Sayer of International Investment Marketing, Allied Dunbar Assurance plc

18.1   Introduction

A life assurance policy is a contract between the individual policy holders and the life assurance company. The life company maintains the underlying investment funds in its own right but, depending on the nature of the policy, it undertakes to pay the policy holder either a specified sum, or a sum which is increased periodically out of the profits of the company, or one which varies from time to time with the value of that part of the underlying fund 'earmarked' for that particular investor. One of the most important characteristics of the life assurance policy as an investment is that it does not produce an income (which would, of course, be exposed to taxation) but is essentially a medium- to long-term accumulator.

Naturally, all life assurance policies provide life cover — a sum assured payable upon death. Most policies, other than temporary assurances, usually also provide investment benefits — sums payable on surrender or maturity of the policy. Life assurance policies may be divided into three categories depending upon the emphasis that is placed on savings or on protection (life cover):

(1)   An endowment policy: has a high savings element and is one under which the benefits are payable at the end of the predetermined period (the endowment term) or on death, if earlier.
(2)   A whole of life policy: one under which the benefits are in general payable on death, whenever it occurs.
(3)   A term policy: a temporary assurance, the sum assured being paid only if death occurs within a specified period.

Term assurances are used entirely for protection against financial hardship on death and will not be considered further here.

18.2 Three types of policy

Within the endowment and whole of life categories the life policies can be one of three different types, depending on the way in which the sums payable by the company are determined:

(1) With profit contracts are policies under which a minimum sum is guaranteed to be paid by the life company on certain specified events, augmented from time to time by bonuses declared by the company according to its profits. These bonuses may be reversionary (bonuses added to the sum assured, either yearly or triennially) or terminal (bonuses declared at the end of the policy as an increment to the final payment).

(2) Without profit contracts are policies under which the life company guarantees, on certain specified events, to pay an absolute sum and invests the premiums in such a way as to produce that sum, bearing any short-fall in the return or retaining any profit in excess of the guaranteed return.

(3) Under unit-linked policies the life company maintains an underlying fund, which is divided, for accounting purposes, into 'units' and undertakes to pay to the policy holder an amount equal to the greater of any guaranteed sum and the value of the units allocated to the policy. The underlying fund might consist of specific types of investment media (such as property, equities, unit trusts, investment trusts, government securities, local authority and bank loans or deposits, or building society deposits) or the fund may consist of a combination of some of all of these ('managed' or 'mixed' funds).

A life company generally has full investment freedom as to the type of investments it chooses, subject only to the investment being a suitable 'match' for its liabilities. In the case of unit-linked policies, the Insurance Company Regulations permit linkage only to certain types of assets, such as those listed above. If the contract is one which incorporates a guaranteed maturity value, the investor knows that he will get at least that sum. At the same time, in the case of with profit policies, he has the advantage of having the guaranteed sum augmented from time to time by reversionary and terminal bonuses. With unit-linked contracts, the value is augmented by the movement of the value of the underlying fund (capital appreciation plus re-invested income).

Life policies can be sub-divided into two main types depending upon how the premiums are payable:

(1) Regular premium policies are those under which premiums are payable annually, half yearly, quarterly or monthly, either throughout the duration of the policy or for a limited premium-paying period. This type of policy is suitable for the regular saver, probably investing out of income, who is looking to amass a capital sum for the future.

(2) Single premium policies, generally known as single premium bonds, are purchased by way of one single premium or lump sum payment. Clearly, they are designed for the capital investor.

18.3   Tax treatment of life assurance policies

The usual logic for making investments through the medium of a life assurance policy is that the proceeds, when taken from the policy, can benefit from advantageous tax treatment in the United Kingdom. The tax treatment of both 'qualifying' and 'non-qualifying' policies is dealt with in more detail in Chapter 4.

It will be seen that, so far as policies issued by a UK company are concerned, the disadvantage to be weighed against the advantage mentioned above is that the life fund in which the investment is being made is itself taxed. Income received and realised gains made by the fund are both taxable. Policies issued by offshore life offices will, in general, not suffer from the taxation disadvantages but neither can they offer an advantageous treatment of proceeds, following the Finance Act 1984 (now incorporated in FA 1988).

The Act, however, provides (Sched 15, para 6), in the case of a regular-payment policy (such as a ten-year endowment policy — the shortest period for which a qualifying policy can be issued) for a special offshore/onshore hybrid where a UK policy is issued in substitution for an offshore policy when and if the policy holder becomes UK resident. Providing that this is done within a year of coming to the United Kingdom, the tax advantages on the taking of proceeds are preserved. Unfortunately, in January 1988 the Inland Revenue announced fundamental changes to its interpretation of contract law as it concerns the exercise of options in life policies, which have effectively removed one of the main advantages of this type of policy. The options specifically attacked by the Revenue are the 'Regular Withdrawal Options' contained in many endowment policies (including the offshore/onshore hybrid type) which enable the policy holder to reduce the premium to a nominal amount (eg £1 a year) and take what is in effect a tax-free income from the policy after a qualifying period, usually ten years. This option was, obviously, particularly attractive to the higher taxpayer. The Revenue action means that it has not been possible to sell such qualifying policies containing such an option since 25 February 1988. Existing policies and offshore/onshore hybrids which were issued before 25 February 1988 are not affected.

The offshore investor seeking to hold his investment through a trust should also note that an offshore life policy written in trust or transferred to non-resident trustees after 19 March 1985 is subject to tax on income on the full gain irrespective of the policyholder's period of non-UK residence, FA 1988.

The two kinds of policies normally considered by investors are the ten-year endowment and single premium bonds. The single premium bond can be considered as an alternative investment to unit or investment trusts and/or offshore funds but investors should note the disadvantageous tax treatment of offshore bonds compared to onshore bonds (see Chapter 4). The ten-year endowment policy can play a useful role in an expatriate's portfolio of investments, provided that the role it is to play is a considered one.

A good financial adviser will look at life assurance in the context of his client's whole life cycle, with regard to his career prospects, that is to say, the need to build up his wealth, pension requirements, dependants' needs, and so on. In other words, life assurance should be viewed as an element — an important one, of course — in the individual's overall asset management, and there is an increasing awareness of this fact among properly competent financial advisers. There are many other aspects of insurance, mainly concerned with the individual's health and unexpected threats to it, but these lie outside the topic of life assurance considered as an investment, which is what we have considered in this chapter.

19 Pensions

Debbie Harrison, Editor, Financial Times Pensions Handbook

Pension planning is one of the more complex areas of personal finance for the British expatriate, and it is a topic that should form part of a comprehensive financial review, rather than being treated in isolation. A point of particular importance is the impact of pension arrangements on the expatriate's position regarding taxation.

In this chapter we aim to provide a basic guide to successful pension planning to two broad categories of expatriate: the employee going overseas on a long-term assignment, and the pensioner planning to spend his or her retirement abroad. We conclude the chapter with a list of useful addresses for those readers who wish to find out more about their current pension options.

19.1 Employees

Pension planning for employees should always start with a detailed analysis of existing provision. This rule applies to everyone, and not just to expatriates, because it is only when the basic building blocks are identified and in place that it is possible to fill gaps in provision and plan for the future.

There are three main sources of pension in the United Kingdom and throughout most of the western world:

(1) state schemes;
(2) occupational schemes; and
(3) private plans.

But while the same three pillars of pension provision can be recognised in other countries outside the United Kingdom, the emphasis between them varies considerably. For example: in the United Kingdom, employees and the self-employed derive the largest proportion of their total pension from occupational schemes and private plans, whereas in Italy and France and many other countries compulsory state schemes provide virtually all of an individual's pension in retirement. In most EC member states, for instance, private individual plans are rare.

19.2 State pensions

Many expatriates ignore their state pension on the false assumption that it does not apply to persons with a peripatetic lifestyle who are also often highly paid. It is true that the UK state pension is not particularly generous — certainly not in comparison with other EC countries — but it forms, nevertheless, a reliable inflation-linked element in an individual's total retirement income.

Few financial advisers fully understand the vagaries of the UK state pension system, and where the eventual pension is multi-source — ie it will be drawn from several countries — it is vital for the individual to keep a good record of contributions paid and benefits due.

In the United Kingdom the state pension consists of two elements — a basic or 'old age' pension and an earnings-related pension. The full rate of the basic pension from April 1992 is £54.15 per week for a single person. Eligibility to the basic pension depends on an individual's National Insurance Contribution (NIC) record.

National Insurance is a form of taxation, and for most employees it is levied at 9 per cent on earnings between an upper and lower limit. These 'band earnings' are earnings between £54 and £405 per week for the 1992/93 financial year.

To qualify for the top rate of pension it is necessary to have paid NICs for a full working career of between 35 and 40 years. Where an individual has less than a full contribution record a proportion of the pension is paid. Women who have not paid enough NICs to entitle them to a pension in their own right can claim a Category B pension under their husband's contributions.

The Category B pension is paid only when the husband reaches state pension age of 65, and not when the wife reaches the state pension age of 60. The Category B pension, which is worth £32.55 per week from April 1992, is added to the husband's single person's pension of £54.15 to give what is known as the married couple's pension, currently worth £86.70.

If a woman is entitled to a small proportion of the basic pension in her own right she can claim this from age 60. Where the Category B pension is worth more, this will be paid when her husband reaches age 65. It is important to remember that the Category B pension replaces and is not paid in addition to the earlier pension.

The second element of the state pension is known as Serps — the State Earnings Related Pension Scheme. Employees automatically belong to Serps if they are not contracted out via an occupational scheme or an 'appropriate' personal pension.

The Social Security Act 1986 reduced the Serps pension for those who retire after the end of the century. Under the original terms of Serps, which was introduced in 1978, the maximum pension was 25 per cent of band earnings assessed over the individual's best 20 years of earnings. However, after 6 April 2000, the 25 per cent maximum will be reduced over a period of ten years to 20 per cent. Also the 'best 20 years' basis of assessment will be replaced by average band earnings over a lifetime. This means that all periods of employment, including periods of low earnings, will be taken into consideration. The overall effect will be to pull down the value of the pension — an important factor for those who expect to rely heavily on their Serps pension.

Few people have a clear idea of what their state pension may be worth. However, the Department of Social Security (DSS) operates a useful pensions forecast service. For details see the contacts list at the end of this chapter.

Fortunately, in most cases, it is possible to continue to build up state retirement benefits when you work abroad. But the rules vary according to the country of employment and the nature of the social security agreement between the foreign country and the United Kingdom.

19.3   EC Multilateral Agreement

The EC, for example, operates the Multilateral Agreement on Social Security. This came into effect following the Treaty of Rome in 1958 which established the European Community. Under the agreement, a UK national can work in different EC countries and continue to build up a right to a state pension from each country through the payment of local national insurance contributions. On retirement the individual can retire anywhere in the Community and draw a pension based on the total number of years worked within the EC.

Under normal circumstances an individual who works abroad would pay local national insurance automatically. There are exceptions to this rule, however: for example, where the period of employment is expected to last less than one year. In this case the individual is retained in the UK social security scheme. Occasionally this period can be extended, but this is rare.

The important feature about the Multilateral Agreement is that it allows employees to aggregate the number of contribution years built up throughout the Community in order to claim a proportion of the state pension in each country of employment. The reason for this feature is that different countries have different qualifying periods for the state pension. For example, in the United Kingdom you have to pay NICs for about ten years before you qualify for a proportion of the basic state pension, although under Serps a benefit is earned from day one. In Italy and Spain, the qualifying period is 15 years, so without the agreement an individual could work for ten years in each of these two countries and not have a right to a state pension.

Under the Multilateral Agreement a pension will be paid from each country of employment provided the *total number* of years worked in the Community exceeds the *minimum qualifying period* in each member state.

On retirement, the pensions are claimed from the relevant country and usually they are paid in the local currency. This means that the pension can be subject to currency fluctuations. Each element of the pension is subject to the annual increases applied by the relevant country. Normally the separate pensions are claimed from each member state but they can be claimed through one source, for example through the equivalent of the DSS in the country of retirement.

The Multilateral Agreement makes no allowance for the fact that different pension ages operate in different member states. This means that a woman can draw her UK state pension from age 60, but will not be able to draw a state pension from Germany until she is 65 and from Denmark until she is 67. At present several EC countries, including the United Kingdom, are expected to equalise their state pension ages for men and women.

19.4   Occupational pensions

Approved occupational schemes and private plans in the United Kingdom are the most tax-efficient method of saving for retirement. Tax relief is awarded on employee and employer contributions up to certain limits, while the funds themselves grow free of income tax and CGT. Moreover, part of the eventual fund can be taken as tax-free cash, although the rest must be taken as pension and is taxed as income.

It is important to bear in mind these tax advantages when considering alternative options. But it is equally important to remember that under an approved UK pension the benefits cannot be taken before age 50 at the very earliest, and for most occupational schemes the normal retirement age is 65 for men, 60 for women.

19.5   Retention in home scheme

Many people who work abroad are seconded by a UK employer and can be retained in the UK company's pension scheme. While the employee may not be able to pay into the scheme if there are no UK 'net relevant earnings', it may be possible for the employee to continue contributions. Because of the tax advantages noted above retention in the home scheme is usually the best option. The normal limit on home country scheme membership for overseas secondment is ten years. The arrangement must be approved by the Pension Schemes Office (PSO).

Where it is not practical or possible to stay in the UK company scheme, the employer should make some provision for pension within the salary package. This should at least match the benefits of the main company scheme.

19.6 Final salary

Most company schemes in the United Kingdom operate on what is known as a final salary or defined benefit basis. This means that for every year of service the employee earns a proportion of his or her final salary up to a maximum pension of two-thirds final salary. The most common pattern is to build up a pension at the rate of $\frac{1}{60}$ of final salary for each year of service up to a maximum after 40 years of two-thirds (ie $\frac{40}{60}$ths) of final salary.

This type of pension offers a valuable hedge against inflation since the pension is linked to the employee's final salary which, under normal circumstances, can be expected to outstrip the RPI.

19.7 Money purchase

Some schemes offer what are known as money purchase pensions. Under a money purchase pension, contributions are invested to provide a fund at retirement which is used to buy an annuity from an insurance company. This means that the retirement income is dependent on the investment performance of the fund and the size of the annuity the fund is able to buy.

Investment performance varies considerably from company to company and annuity rates fluctuate according to the underlying rate of inflation. This does not necessarily mean that money purchase is a poor alternative to final salary, but it does place more emphasis on the careful choice of pension provider, and this should be done with the help of a pensions adviser.

Where an employee is retained in his or her UK company scheme it is important to examine the tax consequences. Many foreign tax authorities will regard the contributions paid by the UK employer as additional salary and will tax these contributions as income. In some countries — France for example — it is compulsory to join the local supplementary schemes known as '*Cadres*'. Under the circumstances it may not be possible or advisable to remain in the UK scheme as well.

19.8 Personal pensions

Personal pensions were introduced in the United Kingdom in 1988 and enabled employees to contract out of Serps for the first time on an individual basis. Unfortunately, it is not possible to continue to pay into a personal pension plan from abroad unless there is a source of UK earned income on which contributions can be based.

If you are planning to go abroad in the near future and would like to take out a personal pension in the meantime then choose the plan carefully. Many people fall into the trap of setting up a monthly premium personal pension plan only to find that there is a hefty financial penalty when it is no longer possible to keep up the payments.

Any planned future changes of employment status should be discussed with a qualified adviser at the outset, so that a suitably flexible plan is selected. If in doubt, it is always sensible to make pension contributions on a single premium basis rather than on a regular basis such as a monthly or annual plan. This avoids any lock-in situation where early termination penalties might apply.

19.9   Pension options abroad

19.9.1   Foreign employer's scheme

If it is necessary to leave the UK company pension scheme when you go abroad it is important to investigate the pensions options available overseas. The most attractive option is likely to be to join the foreign company's pension scheme, as this will probably include the advantage of employer contributions in addition to the employee's own contributions. As in the United Kingdom, most countries award tax relief on contributions to approved pension schemes — an important consideration if you are paying local taxes.

However, there are circumstances when it might not be advisable to join the foreign company's scheme. For example, rather as with state pension schemes, in many countries it is necessary to work for several years before you have what is known as a 'vested right'. The vesting period refers to the number of years you need to be in a company pension scheme before you become entitled to a pre-served pension or transfer value when you leave.

A preserved pension is the pension benefit you leave behind in a former employer's scheme. The benefit, which cannot be drawn until retirement, builds up at a modest rate within the scheme. This pension benefit in most cases can be transferred to another scheme (see **19.11**). However, if you leave before the vesting period is completed, you can end up with nothing to show for your contributions.

In the United Kingdom, employees are entitled to a preserved pension after two years. If an employee leaves a company before then all he or she is entitled to is a return of employee contributions (but not the employer's). Moreover, a deduction is made for back payments into Serps for that period of employment, and on top of this a deduction is made for tax.

The United Kingdom is quite lenient, however, in its vesting rules. In Belgium, for example, the vesting period is five years, while in other countries it is necessary to work for 15 years or more before earning the right to a preserved pension.

19.9.2 Individual plans

Where the foreign employer does not offer a company pension scheme or it is inappropriate to join — perhaps because the job is expected to last for just a few years — the next best choice would be a local private individual plan. The foreign equivalent to personal pensions can be a good choice particularly if contributions attract tax relief at the individual's highest marginal rate. But it is worth noting that the United Kingdom is more advanced in its private pensions market than many other countries.

In the United States and Australia similar plans are available, but in the EC the personal pensions market is underdeveloped. This is mainly because the combination of state and occupational schemes provides a very high level of benefit and there is no need for other types of pension.

Some countries are beginning to develop an individual pensions market in a bid to switch part of the burden of pension provision from the state to the private sector. This is essential if countries are to come to terms with the cost of state schemes as the number of elderly people claiming benefits rises and the number of workers contributing to the schemes falls. For example France, which faces one of the most pressing demographic problems in Europe, in 1990 introduced legislation to establish tax-efficient eight-year personal savings plans to cater for the private pensions market.

The other point to note about an individual plan is that it will not provide the important fringe benefits that a good company scheme offers, such as death benefits and widow's and dependents' pensions. Most company schemes also offer good private medical and long-term disability insurance. If you have to go it alone, make sure your insurance policies cover these important requirements.

19.10   Offshore pensions

Owing to the inflexibility associated with some foreign pension schemes, many expatriates, and particularly those who are constantly on the move, prefer the idea of an offshore pension fund which can be built up from wherever the employment takes place.

Offshore pensions broadly divide into two categories, namely the employer-sponsored offshore trusts, and the individual plans sold by the offshore arms of UK and other EC insurance companies.

19.10.1   Employer-sponsored offshore trust

By far the best arrangement is the employer-sponsored offshore trust. This type of arrangement is commonly used by the large multinationals which need to provide a top quality pensions package to their expatriate executives.

Offshore pension trusts can be tailored to meet the specific needs of the employees. They can cater, for example, for earlier retirement age than the company's main pension scheme — an essential feature for those expatriates who spend their working lives in a highly stressful or dangerous environment or in an unpleasant climate.

The trusts are established in a suitable offshore location. United Kingdom employers tend to prefer the Channel Islands, American companies opt for Bermuda and the Caribbean, German companies go for Liechtenstein or Luxembourg, while for historical reasons the Dutch prefer Curaçao.

Provided the offshore location offers a strong regulatory environment and the services necessary to operate a pension trust, few problems should arise. From the employee's point of view, however, it is essential to have a secure contract setting out the pension benefits in detail. This is important because a pension promise, which is simply a verbal agreement to the employee that the pension will be no less than that provided by the main company scheme, can prove worthless if the company is taken over or if the employee leaves under awkward circumstances.

19.10.2 Individual offshore plans

The scope for good quality offshore individual pension plans is limited, although for the UK expatriate there is a thriving market of offshore insurance companies, based in the Channel Islands and Isle of Man, that offer a range of financial products. Some of these are designed to mirror pension plans in the United Kingdom, but they should never be confused with the real article. The important point to remember with this type of policy is that it simply cannot mirror the tax advantages of an onshore, Revenue-approved UK pension plan, but some plans do offer limited tax advantages and can be transferred to a UK plan if the expatriate returns home.

There is not space here to undertake a detailed analysis of each product, but it is worth pointing out that many offshore plans used for the pensions market are based on ten-year maximum invest-ment plans (MIP) and commit the individual to a long period of regular contributions. If an MIP is selected it is important to check what charges are imposed if, for example, the overseas second-ment is terminated early.

Recent developments in the Channel Islands include the launch of the 'Section 131c' plan for overseas residents and foreign nationals. This type of plan aims to mirror the investment pattern of UK personal pensions, although the plans cannot offer the same tax treatment of contributions and benefits for an expatriate who returns to the United Kingdom.

Expatriates interested in an individual offshore plan suitable for retirement planning should consult a reputable firm of financial advisers specialising in expatriate tax and pension planning. A contact for offshore providers is given at the end of the chapter.

For many expatriates, particularly those on short-term secondment overseas, the most sensible route to retirement planning is to opt for a mixture of offshore investments which provide flexibility and good long-term growth prospects.

19.11 Transfers

So far we have dealt with current and future pension planning, however, it is equally important to consider the pension benefits built up before the individual goes overseas. There are several options for individuals who leave behind a preserved pension when they go overseas, but it must be stressed that the whole issue of pension transfers is fraught with difficulty and calls for the expertise of a professional tax or actuarial adviser.

Cash refund
Where membership of the UK company pension scheme was for less than two years, it is possible to get a cash refund of employee contributions less certain deductions for tax and back payments into Serps.

Preserved pension
In many cases the best option where the pension benefit is substantial is to leave it where it is and to draw a pension from this source in retirement. Before this decision can be made it is important to get a pensions expert to analyse what the former employer's scheme provides in the way of annual increases — both compulsory and discretionary — and dependants' benefits such as widows' and childrens' pensions.

It is also important to check with the scheme trustees if the scheme has a surplus or deficit (this may have a significant impact on the level of indexation of benefits after certain provisions of the 1990 Social Security Act come into force).

A foreign company transfer
If the foreign employer has a pension scheme it is possible in certain circumstances to transfer the value of the UK scheme into the new scheme. This would need careful consideration to ensure that the benefits guaranteed in the new scheme were roughly equal to the benefits being given up in the old scheme. Transfers to foreign schemes are dealt with by the Pension Schemes Office and are permitted only in certain cases. This option is worth considering only where the employee intends to remain abroad and stay with the same company for a long period.

A UK personal pension or buy-out bond
Sometimes it is worth transferring the benefit out of the former employer's scheme and into a personal pension or buy-out bond, both of which are sold by insurance companies, although in the

case of personal pensions other financial institutions such as unit trust groups, banks and building societies also offer products. In some cases such a transfer will yield better results, but it is essential that a pensions expert checks all other options first. This will require a detailed knowledge of the former employer's scheme.

Foreign individual plans
As mentioned above, a growing number of countries now offer an individual personal pension option. Transfers to individual plans overseas are rare, but in special circumstances can be authorised by the overseas branch of the Pension Schemes Office.

19.12 Retiring abroad

For many individuals the prospect of becoming expatriate does not arise until after retirement. In these circumstances pension planning centres around how to get your various pensions sent to your overseas address without incurring any double taxation penalties.

British state pensions can be claimed from anywhere in the world. However, the amount payable is frozen at the date the individual leaves the United Kingdom and cost-of-living increases are paid only if the individual retires to an EC country or to one of the countries with which the United Kingdom has a social security agreement which includes an uprating agreement (see Table 19.1). This means that if you move to Australia or New Zealand, for example, you will not receive the annual increases. Without these increases the value of the pension will rapidly erode. The only good news is that if you subsequently return to the United Kingdom, your pension will be restored to its full current value.

Company pensions in the United Kingdom can be paid to virtually any address abroad with little difficulty. But to avoid the blow of double taxation it is necessary to obtain a declaration from the foreign tax authority stating that you are resident and being taxed on your worldwide income in that country. This must be sent as soon as possible to your UK tax inspector. Without this certificate the UK Inland Revenue will impose a withholding tax of 25 per cent on all pension payments, although this should be repaid once the certificate is through.

The same principles apply to private plans in the United Kingdom, including annuities purchased with retirement annuity contracts and personal pensions.

Table 19.1   Countries with which the United Kingdom has a social security agreement which provides for annual increases

Austria	Ireland	The Netherlands
Belgium	Italy	Norway
Bermuda	Isle of Man	Philippines
Cyprus	Israel	Portugal
Denmark	Jamaica	Spain
Finland	Jersey	Sweden
France	Luxembourg	Switzerland
Germany	Malta	Turkey
Guernsey	Mauritius	United States
Iceland		

19.13   Useful addresses

To find out how much your UK state pension is worth, contact your local DSS and ask for pension forecast form BR19. For specific enquiries about claiming a state pension from abroad contact:

Department of Social Security
Overseas Branch
Newcastle-upon-Tyne
NE98 1YX

If you have difficulty tracing your pension with a former employer contact:

Pensions Register
PO Box 1NN
Newcastle-upon-Tyne
NE99 1NN

Pension complaints initially should be put in writing to the scheme manager, trustees or provider. The next step, if you are dissatisfied with the response, is to contact the Occupational Pensions Advisory Service (OPAS) preferably through the local Citizens Advice Bureau. OPAS can also be contacted direct at:

11 Belgrave Road
London
SW1Z 1RB

Information on offshore product providers is available from:

Offshore Life Offices Association (OLOA)
c/o Richard Gough
Royal Life International
Royal Court
Castletown
Isle of Man

20 The international monetary system

Howard Flight, Managing Director, Guinness Flight Global Asset Management Ltd

20.1 Introduction

The 1990s have seen a compromise develop in the world's exchange rate system since what may be described as the 'free for all' floating exchange rates in operation in the two previous decades. The major currencies — essentially the US dollar, the European currency bloc, and the Japanese yen — continue to operate on the basis of floating exhange rates, where their parities against one another find their own levels on the foreign exchange markets. But for the currencies within the North American and European currency groupings, the relevant exchange rates are now fixed or controlled within certain limits, at least, and in Europe they are pledged to move towards fully fixed exchange rates, en route to a common currency.

The three main international currencies continue to play a dual role: they not only act as standards of value for the purposes of international trade, but they also behave as and are viewed as financial assets in their own right. Particularly in Europe, the extent to which currencies may move against one another within the European Monetary System (see **20.5**) is limited, and over the last five years, as part of the process of moving towards a common currency, realignments within the system have ceased, with elements in the real national economy of any given country (notably interest rates and the labour market) having to bear the adjustment process made necessary by differing inflation rates in the EC member states. The US and Canadian dollars are not subject to any official limitation on their divergence, but the North American Free Trade Agreement effectively requires reasonable currency stability. Within Europe, for the time being at least, there is still scope for exchange rate movements for the separate national currencies within their respective bands in the system. At present, the greatest potential for divergence is between the Spanish peseta and the pound sterling, as both operate on 6 per cent bands. The commitment to a common European currency is now under severe strain as a result of German re-unification. But in spite of the arguments over the Maastricht Treaty, the commitment is likely to be maintained.

20.2   Fixed versus floating exchange rates

20.2.1   Fixed exchange rate system

Until 1931 the world operated on a fixed exchange rate system based on gold, and this exerted an automatic discipline on inflationary tendencies, in whatever country they occurred. But the gold standard, as it was known, broke down in 1931, partly as a result of the political and economic turmoil after the First World War, but also because an international monetary system based on the convertibility of gold into the various national currencies was no longer adequate to accommodate the growing economic complexities of the twentieth century.

As the end of the Second World War came in sight, a meeting under the auspices of the United Nations was held in 1944 at Bretton Woods, New Hampshire, with the aim of devising a satisfactory international monetary system to come into operation when the war ended. The Bretton Woods system attempted to combine the stability of the old gold standard with the demands of post-war recovery. Worldwide inter-tradability of currencies was to be achieved through the elimination of exchange controls, reasonable stability of exchange rates, and full employment.

But as a combination, these three objectives proved incompatible, and within 20 years of its establishment the Bretton Woods system began to break down. The main problem was that the system accommodated inflation by allowing governments to finance their budget deficits by unlimited large-scale borrowing. The fixing of the price of gold at US$33 per ounce also proved unworkable. A factor of equal importance was the huge growth in world trade, which produced a growing build-up in mobile international funds, rendering it increasingly difficult for central banks to manage fixed exchange rates. The final blow to the system was the Vietnam War, which caused private demand for gold to surge, forcing the establishment of a separate free market in gold for the private sector, which had hitherto not been allowed to hold gold, except in the form of jewellery.

20.2.2   Floating exchange rate system

The United States suspended dollar-gold convertibility at $33 per ounce in 1971, unilaterally bringing the Bretton Woods system to an end. After the formal devaluations of the dollar against gold in 1971 and 1973, the major currencies were allowed to float freely. The principle of floating exchange rates is very simple. The exchange rate of each currency is allowed to find its own value in the marketplace, reflecting flows of funds — supply and demand. At the same time, each country's central bank is allowed some scope, depending upon the size of its reserves, to manage its own exchange rates. The floating rate system accommodates and indeed tends to encourage different rates of inflation among the different national economics. On the positive side it also accommodates shocks, such as the oil price rises in the 1970s and local wars, in a relatively painless manner.

There is, however, no self-correcting mechanism in the system to deal with inflation. Thus, after the first oil price hike in 1973, governments reacted generally by competitive devaluation in their attempt to avoid lowering living standards. But inflation in some national economies reached double figures as a result.

The floating exchange rate system also led to increasingly volatile exchange rate movements. This trend, combined with fears of growing inflation, induced governments and central banks to get together in the course of the late 1980s with the objective of managing exchange rates more actively, but still within the floating system.

In the EC it was seen from the outset that floating exchange rates worked against economic and political unity. As early as 1972, continental European governments introduced the so-called 'Snake in the Tunnel' rules restricting currency fluctuations round central rates as a first step towards monetary union, and this developed in 1979 into the European Monetary System (EMS) and the subsequent commitment, formally agreed at the end of 1991 at Maastricht, to a common European currency.

From a practical point of view, although the world continues to operate under a floating exchange rate system, this is now essentially confined to three main currencies or currency blocs — the dollar, the EC, and the yen. While there is still considerable volatility among these three blocs, the extent of the movement from top to bottom within currency cycles is generally smaller than it was during the 1970s and the first half of the 1980s; and it has also led, so far, to rather shorter currency cycles. The present system, of semi-fixed exchange rates within politically and economically related country groupings, but floating rates between these groupings, is likely to continue in operation for a considerable period of time.

This means that for expatriates (or others with exposure to currency fluctuations) the need to worry about exchange rate movements is considerably less within a particular currency bloc, especially the European bloc (even though there is still scope for movement in the 2.25 per cent band for most currencies in the EMS and the 6 per cent band still prevailing, as this Guide goes to press, for the pound sterling and the Spanish peseta).

But for transactions and flows of money between the three main currency blocs, the task of exchange rate management has, if anything, become more difficult. The central banks are both active competitors with and restraints on corporations or private individuals in benefiting from clear, major, and market-driven over- or undervaluation trends. In the short term, potential volatility among the three main currencies is probably higher than it was previously. In this situation, from an international vantage point, there is an overwhelming argument for maintaining a 'managed basket approach' to exchange rate exposure and international cash management.

20.3 Factors driving exchange rate movements

As far as the major international currency blocs still operating under a floating exchange rate are concerned, the important point is to distinguish between the relative long-term trends of strength and weakness, reflecting different levels of inflation, differences in the rate of increase of productivity and in overall international competitiveness, and the shorter-term movements, where there remains a tendency for exchange rates to move in a cyclical pattern along their longer-term trends, caused by international flows of capital. These cycles are driven by a mixture of movements in interest rate differentials, political factors, and the market's view of the relative cheapness and dearness of currencies, particularly with reference to their relative purchasing power in their own home market.

The cycles are not as extreme as they were in the 1970s and early 1980s, partly as a result of intervention in the market by the central banks of the seven major countries (the United States, Japan, Germany, France, Italy, the United Kingdom and Canada), and partly because the marketplace itself has become more experienced. Put simply, the long-term rising and falling trends of particular currencies, determined by international competitiveness, will be reflected in the tendency towards trade surpluses or trade deficits. The shorter-term cycles are entirely about flows of international capital, where for the time being movements and expected movements in interest rate differentials are the most important factor.

20.4   The world's major currencies

We have identified three major currencies or currency blocs at the present time — the US dollar, the European bloc, led by the deutschemark, and the yen. But up until the end of the 1980s, five distinct major currencies were important: the US dollar, the yen, the deutschemark, sterling, and the Swiss franc.

The Swiss franc has lost its previous special role as a strong refuge currency, to become a relatively weak European currency outside the Exchange Rate Mechanism, although it is still related to the deutschemark. It is striking that neither the break-up of the Soviet Union nor the Gulf War served to revive any refuge role for the Swiss franc. Switzerland's present relatively high rate of inflation — above the levels of the United Kingdom and Germany — and the Swiss franc's lower real interest rates have rendered it a relatively weak and unattractive European currency (except to borrow in), and one likely to drift lower against the deutschemark.

Within the dollar bloc the components are the US and Canadian dollars, with the Hong Kong dollar, which is formally tied to the US dollar. In part by virtue of their names, the Australian dollar and the New Zealand dollar have come to be regarded as loosely part of the US dollar bloc. But their divergence from the US dollar in recent years does not, for the time being at least, lend much support to regarding them as US dollar surrogates. Within the North American free trade bloc, Mexico has made great progress in reducing its level of inflation, and the Mexican peso is coming to behave as a dollar bloc currency, subject to modest regular devaluation offset by appropriately higher rates of interest.

In spite of the economic predominance of Japan in Asia, there are as yet no formal or informal links between the Japanese yen and the currencies of the nation states of the region. These are for the most part managed against a basket of international currencies reflecting their respective national economies' trading patterns, and several of them are not freely convertible. With some exceptions, the relatively high rates of inflation in these countries require them to devalue their currencies frequently. The yen, however, has continued to grow in importance as a major world reserve currency.

20.5 The European Exchange Rate Mechanism

With the exception of the Greek drachma, all the currencies of the EC participate in the Exchange Rate Mechanism (ERM). This is the central feature of the EMS, fixing the upper and lower limits beyond which the currencies of EC member states are not allowed to diverge against a fixed central rate calculated against the European currency unit, the Ecu. For most EC currencies, the limits of divergence are 2.25 per cent above or below the central rate; but for sterling, the Spanish peseta, and the Portuguese escudo, the limits are 6 per cent either way. Sterling, however, is expected to come within the narrower band in the near future.

The European currency unit, the Ecu just referred to, is an embryo European currency that came into being in March 1979 as a component of the EMS, originally to serve as a reference point or denominator for the ERM. As such, it is a composite unit artificially constructed from a basket of the 11 EC currencies (the Belgian and Luxembourg francs count as one currency), according to specified amounts. The relative amounts of the component currencies are intended to reflect their respective countries' economic strength in the Community. With a weight of just over 30 per cent of the whole Ecu, the German mark is the most powerful currency in it, followed by the French franc, sterling, the Italian lira, and the Dutch guilder, in that order.

The EMS was formally incorporated in the Treaty of Rome (1957) under the Single European Act, which came into force in July 1987. Under the Treaty of Maastricht (signed in February 1992, but since its rejection by the people of Denmark in a referendum in June 1992, due either for amendment or for replacement by another Treaty), the EC member states are further committed to the establishment of a single European Central Bank on 1 January 1999, which will be responsible for the introduction of a single currency as soon as practicable after that date. A protocol to the treaty, however, states that the United Kingdom 'shall not be obliged or committed to the third stage of economic and monetary union (the adoption of the single currency) without a separate decision to do so by its government and Parliament'.

This is the programme in principle. But in order to be part of the fully-fledged economic and monetary union which the Maastricht Treaty envisages, the member states must meet certain targets regarding inflation, interest rates, exchange rates and public sector debt which have come to be referred to as 'convergence criteria'. The member states are pledged to meet these criteria, but the treaty is not specific as to final deadlines, as distinct from the date of inauguration of the full European central banking system in 1999. Greece particularly, but also Italy and Spain are likely to have difficulties in meeting the criteria. It is also laid down in the treaty that any new EC member states (such as Sweden or Norway) will be eligible for participation in the full economic and monetary union on the same conditions as those that apply to the present member states.

21 Coping with exchange rate movements

Howard Flight, Managing Director, Guinness Flight Global Asset Management Ltd

21.1 Exchange rates and cash: managed currency funds

Especially at times when equity markets have to be approached cautiously, many investors are concerned with managing liquid assets of one kind or another. International investors, including expatriates, must take particular account of the impact of exchange rate movements. But more and more investors are coming to realise that cash (liquidity) investment (in the form of bank deposits or so-called 'financial paper', ie readily negotiable financial instruments) on an international basis represents a major investment opportunity in its own right.

International investment in a managed spread of currencies is the logical approach for multi-currency cash investment, and the managed currency fund was pioneered for this objective by Guinness Flight in 1980. Investors buy shares or units in a fund whose liquid assets are invested in a managed spread normally of the three main currencies or currency blocs identified in the previous chapter, or their component currencies. The spread is changed over a period of time in accordance with the fund managers' assessment of expected exchange rate movements. For each particular currency, assets are held in a mixture of bank deposits, certificates of deposit, floating exchange rate notes and, in some cases where interest rates appear likely to fall, in fixed-interest securities. In broad terms, the investment strategy is to invest in a diversified portfolio of the currencies that are relatively undervalued in terms of economic fundamentals and entering, or soon to enter, bull market cycles, and to avoid undue exposure to currencies that are either in mature bull market cycles or in a phase of long-term declining trend.

There is no doubt that foreign exchange markets can be volatile. To hold cash in one currency only is, from an international perspective, a high-risk or speculative strategy. A diversified and properly managed investment in currencies is the opposite of this — in the short term it will inevitably underperform the strongest currency, although outperforming all currencies over time.

Most managed currency funds (provided there is no element of gearing, whether directly or through unhedged exposure to currency futures) have shown themselves to be highly conservative and bearing a lower risk than either investment in a single specified currency or international investment in equities or bonds. Equities carry higher risks than bonds; and bonds carry higher risks than cash.

21.2 Exchange rates and bonds

The market value of a particular bond is tied to the interest rate (and yield curve, or projection of interest rates over selected periods of time) of the currency in which it is denominated. When interest rates fall, the value of bonds rises, because a larger capital is now needed to yield the same return; and conversely, when interest rates rise, the value of bonds falls.

Under a regime of fixed exchange rates, the only scope for capital gains in bonds depends on the investor's ability to assess the future course of interest rates correctly. But under a system of floating exchange rates, a significant contribution to the total return, measured in the investor's own domestic currency, on investing in bonds internationally will depend on the extent to which the other currencies in which bonds are held either appreciate or depreciate. There are, besides, important links, in more than one context, between the respective movements of exchange rates and interest rates.

The main traditional relationship between exchange rates and bond markets has arisen where particular national bond markets have a large volume of foreign funds invested in them and are thus more influenced than other bond markets by the strength or weakness of the local currency. The sterling gilt market has been a classic example of this, and the strength or weakness of sterling has heavily influenced this market and the interest rates of sterling-denominated bonds generally. The same has applied more and more to the US bond market, where in the 1980s the US government became substantially dependent on attracting flows of foreign funds to finance the US Treasury market. On the other hand, bond markets supplied with funds largely by domestic investors have been traditionally less vulnerable to fluctuations in exchange rates.

But a new and potentially more important contrary relationship has arisen. With interest rate differentials becoming a crucial factor in driving exchange rate movements among the three main currency blocs, there is an increasing tendency for bond markets and exchange rates to move automatically in opposite directions. This is in part because geographical currency groupings reduce the relative importance of wider international financing of bond issues, especially, for example, in the context of Europe.

Broadly speaking, as the market operates at present, if the state of the domestic economy (or group of economies) is likely to lead to lower interest rates, this will drive bond markets up, but it will tend to drive the exchange rate down. Conversely, where the prospective accelerating economic growth is expected to lead to higher interest rates and weaker bond markets, this will drive up the exchange rate.

21.3   Exchange rates and equity investment

Thanks to post-war developments in telecommunications and information technology, the world's main stock markets, like the foreign exchange markets, now operate globally, except in matters of administration. In this environment, exchange rate movements can mean the difference between profit and loss, or, in a stock market crash, the difference between a relatively small loss and a large one. Indeed, profitable international equity investment cannot be achieved unless the exchange rate factor is taken into account in the investor's calculations.

After the worldwide fall in stock markets in October 1987, US investors found that they had suffered less on their foreign investments measured in dollars than investors in other countries measuring their investments in their own currencies. Because the

US dollar fell against the yen, the deutschemark and sterling, shares in the markets in Japan, Germany and the United Kingdom that had been bought with US dollars fell in value much less in dollar terms than in local currency market-value terms, to the extent that the dollar weakened against the currency in question.

Currency weakness is also generally good for the profits and share prices in their local currency terms of companies operating in international sectors (eg export-led sectors). The resulting equity gains, however, will naturally be reduced when measured in the currency of the foreign investor. The expected depreciation of the currencies in question must be included in calculations of comparative projected total investment returns.

For example, an investment in a US company in an international business sector, benefiting from future dollar weakness, may, let us say, be expected to show a 100 per cent return in dollar terms, thus attracting Japanese investors. But if the dollar depreciates by 25 per cent against the yen, the expected return in yen terms will be only 60 per cent. For equities, however, unlike cash and bonds, the positive impact (via profits) of currency depreciation on share prices is often greater for the foreign investor than the accompanying downwards adjustment due to the depreciation.

21.4 Exchange rates and day-to-day living expenses

As pointed out above, the problems and risks for expatriates living in one country but with a flow of income — a pension, for example — denominated in the currency of another country are reduced if both countries are within one and the same major currency bloc. But even within the EC there is still room for considerable fluctuation in the rate of exchange between sterling and the peseta, so that British expatriates who have retired to Spain on a UK pension have been and can still be exposed, for certain periods at least, to a potentially embarrassing risk of the peseta rising against sterling, and so reducing the value of their pension in Spain.

A potentially far greater problem arises, however, when income and living expenses are in two distinct currency blocs, as might be the case, for example, for a retired United Nations official living in France and drawing a pension denominated in US dollars. If it is practical, the only route to protection here is to cover, by means of forward exchange contracts with your bank, your known flow of income in the source currency into the currency of the country where you are living. If this is not a practical option, it may be prudent to keep a reasonable balance on deposit in the currency of the country where you are resident as a reserve to draw on when needed. This tactic can be particularly useful in dealing with temporary weakness in the source currency: you can then postpone converting the income concerned until the currency is stronger.

Appendix I   Checklists of do's and don'ts

Going abroad

One of the most daunting things about going abroad to work is gathering together all the information necessary. Obviously the intending expatriate needs full details of his contract, health, visa and permit requirements and many more. On the financial front, the following are some of the most important things to consider:

(1) *Do* bring your UK tax affairs up to date;
(2) *Do* submit a P85 and claim any PAYE rebate if leaving part way through the tax year;
(3) *Do* inform the Department of Social Security, check if any contributions will be necessary and, if not, obtain an application form for voluntary contributions;
(4) *Do* make arrangements for offshore banking (including a current account for remaining UK commitments and a small amount in a deposit account);
(5) *Do* close any building society deposit accounts;
(6) *Do* inform any mortgagee that the mortgaged property is being left vacant, or if it is to be let, ask his permission;
(7) *Do* check the continuing validity of all protective insurances, both life and personal effects, property, etc;
(8) *Do* take legal advice on letting property;
(9) *Do* make or revise a will;
(10) *Do* review existing investments not already mentioned;
(11) *Do* consider comprehensive insurance protection while overseas;
(12) *Do* make use of duty-free facilities in purchasing a car or household appliances if appropriate;
(13) *Do* inform bankers, solicitors, accountants and other advisers of the new address;
(14) *Do not* leave everything to the last minute;

(15)   *Do not* take on any new investment commitments just before leaving;
(16)   *Do not* forget that most countries are happy to let money in but may impose restrictions on taking it out again — check the rules;
(17)   *Do not* leave valuables at home;
(18)   *Do not* expect to have a large cash surplus, at least in the first few months.

While overseas

Given that earning and saving money is a prime motive in working abroad, many expatriates are very disappointed to find that after six months they have yet to amass a fortune. In retrospect it is hardly surprising. Even the fully furnished company house is usually missing much essential equipment, there can be a great deal of entertaining to be done either at home or at the club, the cost of living until experience of local produce and markets is gained is invariably high, and, after all, a new video and hi-fi are essential.

Usually after about six months, a regular savings or cash surplus pattern can be discerned and at that point some serious consideration can be given to investment.

(1)   *Do* invest surplus cash initially in a readily realisable form such as a very short-term bank deposit;
(2)   *Do* retain an adequate cash reserve;
(3)   *Do* wait until a regular pattern of surplus appears before entering into any major investment commitments;
(4)   *Do* examine all investment propositions very carefully;
(5)   *Do* seek independent advice on all financial matters;
(6)   *Do not* be tempted by tales of massive profits just waiting to be made, at least until a reasonably secure base has been built up;
(7)   *Do not* sign any investment document or part with cash as a result of a brief meeting with a salesman of whose credentials you are not absolutely certain;
(8)   *Do not* make any long-term commitments based on current earning capacity unless that capacity is extremely secure (for most expatriates, it is not);
(9)   *Do not* attempt to beat currency or tax regulations, as the penalties can be extremely severe;
(10)   *Do not* neglect to plan.

Coming home

One of the most vital occasions for tax and investment planning is in the months before returning to the United Kingdom. Much of what has been achieved in terms of savings and investment can be largely undone by a lack of forethought at this point. Amid the round of farewell parties, packing up and thinking of home, it is often very easy to forget to close a bank account or to realise accrued gains. The secret is to plan.

(1) *Do* seek professional advice at least three months before the return date (or if the overseas period is unlikely to last, or to have lasted for at least three years, get advice in the tax year prior to return);
(2) *Do* check any local requirements for tax clearance before the issue of exit visas;
(3) *Do* check current exchange control regulations;
(4) *Do* close all offshore deposit accounts (and in the tax year before return close any UK bank deposit accounts);
(5) *Do* consider CGT and UK income tax liabilities on existing investments;
(6) *Do* give notice to any tenants at home to quit;
(7) *Do* read Chapter 12 again.

Appendix II   Tax tables

Income tax rates for 1992–93 and the previous five years

For 1987–88:

Slice of income	Rate	Total income (after allowances)	Total tax
£17,900 (0–17,900)	27%	£17,900	£4,833
2,500 (17,901–20,400)	40%	20,400	5,833
5,000 (20,401–25,400)	45%	25,400	8,083
7,900 (25,401–33,300)	50%	33,300	12,033
7,900 (33,301–41,200)	55%	41,200	16,378
Remainder	60%		

For 1988–89:

Slice of income	Rate	Total income (after allowances)	Total tax
First £19,300	25%	£19,300	£4,825
Remainder	40%		

For 1989–90:

Slice of income	Rate	Total income (after allowances)	Total tax
First £20,700	25%	£20,700	£5,175
Remainder	40%		

For 1990–91:

Slice of income	Rate	Total income (after allowances)	Total tax
First £20,700	25%	£20,700	£5,175
Remainder	40%		

For 1991–92:

Slice of income	Rate	Total income (after allowances)	Total tax
First £23,700	25%	£23,700	£5,925
Remainder	40%		

For 1992–93:

Slice of income	Rate	Total income (after allowances)	Total tax
First £2,000 (0–2,000)	20%	£2,000	£400
21,700 (2,001–23,700)	25%	23,700	5,825
Remainder	40%		

Income tax personal reliefs for 1992–93 and the previous five years

	1987–88	1988–89	1989–90	1990–91	1991–92	1992–93
Personal: single	£2,425	£2,605	£2,785	—	—	—
Personal: married man	£3,795	£4,095	£4,375	—	—	—
Personal (each)	—	—	—	£3,005(1)	£3,295(1)	£3,445(3)
Married couple	—	—	—	£1,720	£1,720	£1,720
(monthly reduction in year of marriage)	£114$\frac{1}{6}$	£124$\frac{1}{6}$	£132$\frac{1}{2}$	£143$\frac{1}{3}$	£143$\frac{1}{3}$	£143$\frac{1}{3}$
Wife's earned income: max. relief (100% of earnings)	£2,425	£2,605	£2,785	—	—	—
Age allowance						
Reduced by £2 for every £3 of income over	£9,800	£10,600	—	—	—	—
Reduced by £1 for every £2 of income over	—	—	£11,400	£12,300	£13,500	£14,200
65 to 79 (to 1988–89) or to 74 (from 1989–90) in year:						
personal — single	£2,960	£3,180	£3,400	—	—	—
personal — married man	£4,675	£5,035	£5,385	—	—	—
personal (each)	—	—	—	£3,670	£4,020	£4,200
married couple	—	—	—	£2,145	£2,355	£2,465
Maximum income —						
wife or single	£10,602	£11,462	£12,630	£13,630	£14,950	£15,710
husband	£11,120	£12,010	£13,420	£14,480(2)	£16,220(2)	£17,200(2)
80 (to 1988–89) or 75 (from 1989–90) or over in year:						
personal — single	£3,070	£3,310	£3,540	—	—	—
personal — married man	£4,845	£5,205	£5,565	—	—	—
personal (each)	—	—	—	£3,820	£4,180	£4,370

married couple	£2,505	£2,395	£2,185	—	—	—
Maximum income —						
wife or single	£16,050	£15,270	£13,930	£12,910	£11,657	£10,767
husband	£17,620	£16,620	£14,860	£13,780	£12,265	£11,375
Housekeeper	—	—	—	—	abol	£100
Additional relief for children	£1,720	£1,720	£1,720	£1,590	£1,490	£1,370
Widow's bereavement	£1,720	£1,720	£1,720	£1,590	£1,490	£1,370
Dependent relative	—	—	—	—	abol	£100
Woman claimant other than wife	—	—	—	—	abol	£145
(reduced by excess of relative's income over basic retirement pension)	—	—	—	—	—	(£2,045)
Depending on services of son or daughter	—	—	—	—	abol	£55
Blind persons (each)	£1,080	£1,080	£1,080	£540	£540	£540
Capital gains tax						
Annual exemption: Individuals	£5,800	£5,500	£5,000	£5,000	£5,000	£5,000

(1) Transitionally, for husband under 65 with wife at 5.4.90 born pre-6.4.25 £3,400; born pre-6.4.15 £3,540.
(2) Different if wife in higher age bracket than husband.
(3) Transitionally, for husband under 65 with wife at 5.4.90 born pre-6.4.15 £3,540.

Appendix III   Useful addresses

Inland Revenue offices

Inland Revenue Headquarters
Somerset House
Strand
London WC2R 1LB

Tel: (071) 438 6622

Inland Revenue Claims
   Branch
Foreign Division
1st Floor
St John's House
Merton Road
Bootle
Merseyside L69 9BL

Tel: (051) 922 6363

Inspector of Foreign
   Dividends
Lynwood Road
Thames Ditton
Surrey KT7 0DP

Tel: (081) 398 4242

Inland Revenue Head
   Office (Public
   Departments)
Foreign Section
Ty-Glas
Llanishen
Cardiff CF4 5ZD

Tel: (0222) 753271

National Insurance

DHSS Overseas Branch
Newcastle-upon-Tyne
NE98 1YX

Tel: (091) 213 5000

Investor protection: United Kingdom

Securities and Investment
  Board
Gavrelle House
2–14 Bunhill Row
London EC1Y 8RA

Tel: (071) 638 1240

Financial Intermediaries,
  Managers and Brokers
  Regulatory Organisation
  (IMRO)
Broadwalk House
5 Appold Street
London EC2A 2LL

Tel: (071) 628 6022

Life Assurance and Unit
  Trust Regulatory
  Organisation
Centre Point (LAUTRO)
103 New Oxford Street
London WC1A 1QH

Tel: (071) 379 0444

The Securities and
  Futures Authority (SFA)
The Stock Exchange
London EC2N 1EQ

Tel: (071) 256 9000

Offshore centres: supervisory authorities

The Bahamas:
Office of the Registrar
  General
Rodney E Bain Building
Shirley & Parliament
  Streets
PO Box N-532
Nassau

Tel: 1 809 322 3316

Guernsey:
Guernsey Financial
  Services Commission
Valley House
Hirzel Street
St Peter Port

Tel: 44 481 712706

Isle of Man:
Financial Supervision
  Commission
PO Box 58
1–4 Goldie Terrace
Douglas

Tel: 44 624 62487

Jersey:
Economic Adviser's Office
Cyril Le Marquand House
The Parade
St Helier

Tel: 44 534 79111

Index

Other titles in the Allied Dunbar Library

Allied Dunbar Tax Guides

- Allied Dunbar Business Tax and Law Guide — WI Sinclair & John McMullen
- Allied Dunbar Capital Taxes and Estate Planning Guide — WI Sinclair & PD Silke
- Allied Dunbar Investment and Savings Guide 1992–93 — General Editor: Harry Littlefair
- Allied Dunbar Retirement Planning Guide — Barry Bean, Dr Beric Wright & Bill Tadd
- Allied Dunbar Pensions Guide — AM Reardon
- Allied Dunbar Tax Guide — WI Sinclair

All of these titles in the Allied Dunbar Library are available from leading bookshops

For more information please contact: Longman Law, Tax and Finance, 21–27 Lamb's Conduit St, London WC1N 3NJ Tel: (071) 242 2548